Potted Gardens

Potted Gardens

A FRESH APPROACH TO CONTAINER GARDENING

REBECCA COLE

PHOTOGRAPHS BY RICHARD FELBER

Clarkson Potter/Publishers
New York

Published by Clarkson Potter/Publishers, 201 East 50th Street, New York, New York 10022. Member of the Crown Publishing Group.

Random House, Inc.   New York, Toronto, London, Sydney, Auckland

CLARKSON N. POTTER, POTTER, and colophon are trademarks of Clarkson N. Potter, Inc.

http://www.randomhouse.com/

Printed in China

Library of Congress Cataloging-in-Publication Data is available upon request

ISBN 0-517-70457-9

10   9   8   7   6   5   4   3   2   1

First Edition

To Funny Grandpa and Mom

just a few months after my traumatic move to New York City, my mother, worried and helpful, suggested I join a neighborhood gardening group to let a plot of land and make some new friends. As usual I didn't listen to her, and instead took an extra

Rowe, Curt, Ellie, Jarrard, Jeff, Mary Bess, Meg and Tim Cole, Dan Bryant, Daphne Mowatt, Marilyn Reed, Tish and Jim O'Neill, Nancy Hurley, Bob Foster, Bob, Louisa, and Tim Miner, Peg Furness, Joanna Going, Cynthia Penney, Katrina Nieman, Ronnie Eldridge, Betty and Vin-

Acknowledgments

ten years to adjust my country soul to this city life. My mother sadly did not live long enough to see any part of the business of Potted Gardens, but she is certainly responsible for germinating the first seeds.

So many people generously opened their homes, barns, attics, gardens, and businesses to make this book possible, and I am exceedingly grateful to them all. Thank you Aunt Timmy and Uncle Bob Nolan, Fran and Walter Bull, Michael Trapp, Victor Nelson, Debbie

cent Blaine, Edna and Berk Wildman, Mary Lou Blaine, Michael Gerdowsky, Corey Daniels, Lynn Lerner, Jim Allman, Dale Richard and Eric Justian, and Steve and Marcello of The Lively Set.

A special thank you to Dad and Martha for infusing my dreams with practical support. To Mark Simpson, who generously shared his wisdom and bluntness to start me on my way. To the very best friends a gal could ever wish for in times of need: Laurie Arbeiter, Cara Paladino, and Rochelle Ritacco. Anne Northrop and Diana

Burton, thank you from the bottom of my heart.

To Anne Raver, Topher Delaney, James Baggot, and Pheobe Eaton, who plucked me out of near obscurity, I will you all my lost leisure time.

Most of the flowers not grown by Mother Nature for this book were grown by the next best thing: Carvalho and Hodgson Farms at the Union Square Greenmarket in New York City, Bissett and Atlantic Nurseries, and Sterling Gardens in Columbia, South Carolina. To Douglas Joslin, whose boundless wisdom in gardening and antiques enriches this book and my store.

Thank you to my inspirational comrades Susie Benarcik, Gloria Sanchez, and Todd Schrock inspired and created some of the most beautiful potted gardens I have ever seen. Allison MacNamara, Amy Wanggaard, Chris Nahas, and Anita Gravine brought organization, cre-

ativity, and sanity to this project in the perfect doses.

Thanks to the whole team at Stark Design. And to Robbin Gourley, a true kindred spirit, thank you for your passion and artistry.

Thank you to the feisty, fiery Elyse Cheyney, for seeing a book in me before anyone else. And Lauren Shakely, my editor, who weeded and mulched with the flourish and care of a true gardener.

Richard Felber, the greatest, quirkiest photographer imaginable, thank you for making my gardens soar. Your humor, passion, and artistry made this journey even more remarkable. And Nancy Blaine, who gives books their heart for a living, championed and read every draft for love and no money. Thank you for watering my plants and nourishing my soul. My book and my life is better for you being in both.

contents

history

D FARMS

to say that my grandfather taught me how to garden is a good old Irish stretch. The truth is, I paid as little attention to his gardening methods and his garden as I did to my home-

work. Each summer I would arrive in New Hampshire, to play in the three-story tree house, fish in the pond, and live on penny candy from the old country store. The rose gardens, with all their thorns and potential chores, were more of a burden than a joy. The White Mountains looming near, and the forest of birch and pine just beyond the stone wall and the pond, half covered with lilies and green muck, were the garden of my perfect childhood summers. A large, beautiful, sometimes brutal garden.

My grandparents, John and Ruth McQuade, fondly known as "Funny Grandpa and Lady Grandma," are all dressed up and ready to prune their rose garden in Moultonboro, New Hampshire.

ABOVE: **A brief moment of summer repose. My brothers Jeff, Tim, and Curt, and I (in the pigtails) share with cousins Wendy and Julie. On the same summer porch thirty years later,** OPPOSITE. **I reminisce about gardens gone by.**

Childhood Memories

I attribute my passion for gardening to Harvey, my grandfather's hired hand. Harvey was a young man with a wry New Hampshire accent so thick I thought he was born in another country. He and my grandfather worked side by side tending ten large raised beds and five separate gardens. Harvey was deathly allergic to bee stings. Since only seconds stood between the sting, the injection, or death, his epinephrine and a needle were placed in three or four locations around the property. Even as a child I was aware that Harvey risked his life daily to tend the beauty of a garden, yet my memory is that he was always smiling.

Today I share their love and a quarter of their knowledge of the garden. I have been told there is no talking to me when I am in a garden. Something happens to my hearing.

Oddly enough, my grandparents' vast library of literature, art, and architecture included no garden books. For a stubborn Irishman, every gardening problem had a practical solution. Invention was my grandfather's greatest fertilizer. When the rocky soil of northern New England proved too much for young seedlings, the screen door would come off the back of the house. He would reinforce the sides with 2 x 4s and sift hundreds of pounds of soil through the screen like flour for a cake. He "staked" his 10-foot tomato plants from above by securing them to a clothesline and placed pieces of a broken mirror in the soil to reflect the warmth of the sun and thereby lengthen the short New Hampshire growing season. I don't know where he learned his idiosyncratic techniques—over the counter at the feed store or at church on Sunday. Or perhaps he just made it all up as he went along. Like my grandfather, I approach gardening pragmatically—every problem has a solution.

My grandfather's work shed, a converted two-car garage, held a tremendous fascination for me. He cherished each gardening implement, bestowing the same respect on a hoe that a chef affords her prize carving knife. Every tool was artfully displayed, perfectly kept, and never replaced. My grandfather had 300 tools if he had one, but none did the job of another. Each container of recycled tin, wooden crate, or galvanized pail held a different size nail, stake, or twine and was impeccably maintained and efficiently marked for its new purpose. The wooden boxes had once held cereal or ammunition. The pails and tins advertised baked beans or paint or maple syrup. Many had come from my great-grandfather's general store in Manchester, New Hampshire, at the turn of the century. My grandfather's love for the beauty of his tools and makeshift containers influenced my gardening style most. I emulate his artful and thrifty ingenuity in my gardens today.

My great-grandfather Doyle McQuade was a farmer who immigrated to this country from Ireland in the late 19th century. For his family, gardening was a necessity rather than a luxury. On their small plot of land outside of Manchester, every inch was cultivated to feed five people. Doyle's son, my grandfather, left the farm as an adult and prospered in business. After he retired, his gardening interests focused on dozens of raised beds filled with enormous dahlias, 5-foot alliums, and 50 varieties of roses, with only a modest vegetable plot yielding just enough to garnish salads in the summer and supplement the weekly store-bought groceries.

My parents, who lived with four children in rural Pennsylvania on the edge of the encroaching suburbs, leaned more toward purely decorative gardens: my father grew two varieties of roses in one neat row lining the driveway, and my mother planted pansies around the mailbox and fuchsia in pots marking the path to our front door.

When I moved to Chicago, I grew rosemary in a tobacco tin on my windowsill. In New York City, I spent ten years looking for an apartment that would provide more gardening space than a small ledge. On my rooftop terrace overlooking the backyards of Greenwich Village, I now grow a sort of makeshift cottage garden in garbage cans, rusty tins, and old milk crates discarded on the streets of New York.

My family history tells the story of gardening in small spaces: each generation found a way to till the soil by adapting the environment to their needs. Though I gratefully do not need to grow my own vegetables to feed myself, I do grow my own garden to nourish my soul.

Urban Garden, Country Soul

Even though I have now spent more of my life surrounded by soot and sirens than not, I remain a nature-loving country girl at heart. Without an inch of land to my name, I have embraced potted gardening in order to defy my urban environment and still contain some of the nature of a happy childhood.

Before long, I opened a little store in Greenwich Village and also called it Potted Gardens. Wonderful antiques, old junk, cut and potted flowers, seeds, and assorted treasures for the garden and home from all over the world are crammed in the store, but my favorite part about it is the quirky, fascinating people I meet. Kindred spirits from all over the globe have discovered this tiny oasis in downtown Manhattan. Rarely a morning goes by that an old tin, enamel pot, or wooden box isn't left anonymously on the store's front step to become a potted garden by the afternoon. Some of my very best ideas have come from my customers' stories, of cactus gardens in cowboy boots or old pedestal sinks overflowing with ivy in living rooms.

The success of Potted Gardens has been overwhelming in just a few short years. I now spend far more time in other people's gardens than I do in my own. Some of my closest friends suspect that I began this business because I ran out of space to garden. Others speculate that it had more to do with justifying my insatiable appetite for collecting old things. Whatever the reason, Potted Gardens now has a life all its own, recycling pieces of our past and championing the creative gardening spirit in us all.

imagine

a garden is a place where much more than a seed can grow. It is a place of solace, exploration, and experimentation. It is the place where imagination grows.

A flower holds the chaos of the world in a moment of spellbinding beauty. The great anarchist revolutionary Emma Goldman surrounded herself with as many flowers as she did intellectuals. She often felt the former to be the true arbiter of revolutionary spirit. When asked by comrades why she would spend her sparse earnings on flowers rather than on "the cause," she would reply, "This is 'the cause.'" It is impossible to look at a flower with an enemy and think about war.

Tiny orange zinnias, linearis, ABOVE, rise from an old cake tin. OPPOSITE: Purple trachelium gracefully edges a foggy lake.

There Is a Garden in Your Path

A garden is as necessary to the human spirit as water and food are. It is an ostentatious affirmation of the cycle of life and death. The difference between living with a garden and living without one is tremendous. A garden focuses the spirit, brings together friends and family, stimulates creativity, calms the nerves, rejuvenates the body, develops responsibility, and nurtures the soul. I believe it is the essential ingredient to a happy home.

Ironically, just when we need gardens most, more and more of us have moved to smaller homes and apartments and have less and less space in which to garden. At the same time, the pace of our lives has increased to such a degree that it has become more difficult to take the time to smell the roses, never mind grow them. Traditional gardening—growing plants from seeds and cuttings, designating large spaces as "the garden" and filling every inch with a mix of shrubs, perennial flowers, and annual color—is no longer an option for many gardeners.

A potted garden creates drama and design by using containers for a large part of the visual interest and by incorporating far fewer plants than would be necessary in a traditional inground garden. With simple designs and careful plant choices, the labor and cost can be substantially less, although a potted garden can also be taken to a grand scale, costing a bundle initially and requiring an enormous financial and time commitment. The possibilities are limitless.

With a potted garden, each container is a garden in itself. A potted garden can be as tiny and simple as grass seed planted in a cigar box or a geranium in a coffee tin. Place a tin on a kitchen windowsill, and suddenly dishwashing becomes a bit less dreary. Plant 300 containers so that a rooftop blooms year-round, and you have created a miracle in the sky, or it can be as grand as a landscaped terrace.

"Grass" of milk, RIGHT, would be the only carton permitted to remain on Mom's dinner table. Hostas and ornamental grasses create a flower bed, OPPOSITE, inside the store.

that few would consider worthy of cultivation.

Limitations of space, money, and horticultural knowledge need not deter your gardening dreams. Potted gardening will provide endless possibilities to even the most novice among us. Using containers, you can garden anywhere, anytime—indoors and outdoors, in large spaces and small.

Gardening with a Sense of Humor

Gardening, like personality and clothes, should be worn loosely, with plenty of room for laughs. Try not to take your garden too seriously, lest you set yourself up for tremendous frustration and disappointment. As you plan

Necessity, the Mother of Container Gardening

Many hard, tiny, earthless spaces have inspired centuries of gardeners to heights of ingenuity. In Mexico, tin cans and rubber tires hold sandy soil in place for a few flowering succulents. In Italy, terra-cotta pots adorn the steps of nearly every home in every town. In Austria, as if by law, each window is graced with a flowering ledge. In Greece, bougainvillea thrives in every size olive urn and oil can, trellising every arch along every path. In Japan, the bonsai garden transforms the smallest crowded spot into magical serenity.

For some, gardening is thought to be a luxury. For others, it is a means of survival. Without it life can look black and white. With it, one can breathe deep and dream. It is this that inspires me to create gardens out of spaces

what plants to incorporate and how to arrange them, remember that a garden is a place to live, not just a place to work. When choosing flowers and containers, look for humor as well as history and design. It will be hard to be unhappy if your garden makes you smile. Consider poppies blooming in an old piss pot or daffodils poking through the roof of a dilapidated dollhouse. If you live in the city and miss the suburbs, sow some grass seed in a suitcase and consider what you would be giving up if you moved back. When a sense of whimsy predominates, the death of

Ranunculus, RIGHT AND BELOW RIGHT, **daylilies,** FAR RIGHT, **and tulips and hyacinths,** BELOW, FAR RIGHT, **live weeks longer potted than the same flowers would in a cut arrangement. Cut sunflowers,** CENTER RIGHT, **and potted petunias,** BELOW, CENTER RIGHT, **highlight old oilcans and a milk crate. Whimsy, gazania, herbs, and imagination,** FOLLOWING PAGES, **take this truck garden on the road.**

a flower will never feel harsh, but if you expect too much from your garden, disappointment will seep in with the weeds. And like a cat, your garden knows when you're nervous.

Indoor gardening particularly must be done with a chuckle. Without the proper greenhouse environment (which most of us do not have and cannot afford), it is nearly impossible to keep plants flowering, bug free, fed, and properly watered year in and year out. Some potted gardens should be treated like cut-flower arrangements— exquisite and short-lived. But in almost every case a planted flower will last longer than any cut flower no matter how unsuitable the environment. Besides, a potted garden of tulips for a centerpiece will provide two weeks more pleasure than those same tulips cut and placed in a vase.

design

the best teacher of garden design is Mother Nature. She has an inimitable way of placing flowers, weeds, trees, water, rocks, and hills together. No book, school, nursery, or landscaper could improve on a garden she designs. For garden inspiration, look closely at the details of the natural world. Straying too far from nature's teachings can result in thousands of strip malls, endless green grass lawns, and plastic flowers presented as a viable alternative to the real thing. In the garden, "unnatural" plantings are not only less appealing to the eye, they are also harder to maintain.

For many springs, I have rented a house on a beautiful little island off the coast of

Inspiration is best found amid the bald cypress, OPPOSITE. **"Love lies bleeding" (amaranths) in a nail keg at the edge of a dock on Golden Pond,** ABOVE, **and on pages 40 and 41.**

the Outer Banks of North Carolina. As the fishing village has grown more prosperous with tourism, homeowners have taken to sowing grass seed in the sand in front of their cottages. Year after year I watch the hopeless effort to maintain and encourage each blade to grow. Three years after the first seed sprouted in front of my rented home, the "lawn" still looked like an adolescent's first beard. The extraordinary natural beauty of the island boasts hundreds of varieties of grasses, thorny shrubs, and wildflowers that thrive in the salt air, sun, wind, and rain. Smooth sandy beaches with a few wild grasses and gnarled low trees make front lawns far more suited to the setting than a struggling patch of grass.

Developing a Personal Style

Gardening is a great outlet for expressing personal taste and style. Since there are as many possibilities as there are gardeners, there is little reason to follow an arbitrary rule, such as planting colorful annuals in straight rows from shortest to tallest, front to back. Or leaving 12 feet of vinca vines hanging ridiculously below a windowsill garden. Who invented the standard of growing dracaena in the middle of a terra-cotta pot surrounded by a circle of geraniums and finished off with an assorted mix of annuals in every color of the rainbow? When planning your potted garden, abandon any insecurity or inexperience that erodes your personal sense of style, design, or horticultural knowledge.

When we lose our breath rounding a bend in a road that reveals a mountain of wildflowers, we know we've seen beauty. It is that observation that puts us in touch with our own aesthetic. Nurturing our sensitivity to beauty in the world is what allows us to form a personal style. That personal style, mixed with a bit of knowledge and time, is the recipe for a spectacular and original garden.

Some people seem to be born with exquisite taste and sense of design; everyone is born

A textured juxtaposition is created, OPPOSITE, with a phalaeonopsis planted inside burlap and wood. RIGHT: Splendor is found in this blooming dwarf pennisetum grass.

with some degree of these qualities. If you feel they are lacking in your own life, try slowing down enough to truly absorb the things that take your breath away or that make you smile. Before planting your garden, put down your gardening books, magazines, and plant catalogs, and nurture your own good taste by admiring nature. Observe the subtle color combinations of the many greens in the woods. Notice that the sky is seldom true blue and that water varies from green to purple to yellow to black. Note how rarely nature introduces a whole new color; she generally works with a very tight palette. Watch how slight changes in light alter color dramatically. Where light is abundant, colors are naturally brighter and more vivid; in the North or in the shade, blues and greens dominate.

Study the architecture of the natural order of things. Often height and depth are subtly altered with slow gradations. Steep, abrupt alterations are rare and extremely dramatic. Most of nature has soft edges with sharp contrast in light. Tremendous differences in size and scale are gently intermingled. The tallest mountain holds the smallest trees. A tiny buttercup carpets an acre of meadow.

life. If you are not one of the few fortunate enough to garden in a spot that offers more than one or two of these elements, you can reproduce them in miniature. Container gardening is a great way to create a small-scale model of natural wonders.

When planning a potted garden, pay close attention to the way nature contains some of

her bravest work. Notice the small patch of green moss and sedum growing out of a spoonful of soil on the steep slope of a hill, secured by a few random rocks. An exquisite wild container garden! In the city, look at the way a few blades of grass force themselves out of a crack in the pavement. No garden could be bolder! A field of poppies is contained by a wooded forest bordering all sides, and a water lily just skims the pond.

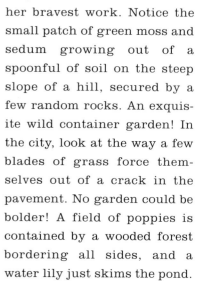

As long as nature guides your gardening, you will never be dissatisfied with the result. Even as one flower dies, a new plant begins to thrive. Nature invented experimentation as a means of survival, and all gardening is an experiment. Although much horticultural knowledge can be learned from books and school, your best teacher is beyond the back door. Study nature for hours, days, weeks, years. Not a moment will be wasted and you will never graduate.

Containing Nature

Nature rarely uses flowers alone to create her gardens. She depends on rocks, hills, ravines, caves, gorges, deserts, mountains, oceans, lakes, and streams to contain the proper growing environments for her diverse plant

Containers are the mountains and streams of potted gardening. Rather than trying to conceal the containers in your garden, choose ones that enhance the beauty of the plants and intrigue the garden observer. Use a variety of containers to add color, texture, height, and depth to your garden. Be inventive. Terra cotta, plastic pots, and redwood boxes can be found in nearly every garden from coast to coast. Instead, forage for containers that express your individuality.

Not long ago the containers that held food in the grocery store were handmade out of

OPPOSITE: **Clerodendrum Thomsoniae pours out of an old Virginia Dare coffee can. Vermont sap bucket,** RIGHT, **blends beautifully with stone steps.** PREVIOUS PAGES: **Rosemary flourishes,** LEFT, **in an old toolbox and verbena bonariensis thrives in a crock,** RIGHT.

wood or tin and artfully painted with bold decorative script proclaiming their contents. It was a time when no two toys were alike, when furniture was painted each year to keep it looking new, and when a tool was forged by hand and its practicality was rivaled only by its graceful lines. An old piece of Americana may no longer serve its original purpose, but the relics of our past, with their simplicity and rustic charm, need not be discarded or placed high on a shelf to collect dust. To make a garden in an old wooden Jell-O box not only displays a piece of nature but also celebrates a bit of history.

Sadly, recent generations have not wanted their homes to look like the homes of their ancestors. Pieces of our history have been all but lost. The magnificent architecture of Europe, the natural beauty of Africa, the startling color of Central and South America, the exquisite environmental design of Asia, the respect for nature of the original Americans have been overtaken by an aesthetic predicated on a desire for new, shiny, easy, and fast.

Potted gardening is one of the ways we can become rooted in our history again. Although many of us will not be able to grow the plants our ancestors did, we may be able to use containers that remind us of days gone by. A country that honors and preserves the diversity of its people and its natural resources is a great country. With nature as our guide, we can clean out our attics and reclaim the relics of our magnificent cultural past.

Color

Color is a crucial aspect of any garden design. There are no bad colors in nature, but there are some pretty dreadful man-made color combinations. Look to the natural world around you for your garden color chart. Keep in mind the old adage "Too much of a good thing . . . ." Putting too many colors in too small a space is a common gardening mistake. Whether for a full garden or an individual potted garden, the tighter the palette, the more successful and natural the design.

I once taught a class on container gardening. A student called me about two months after she had attended the class, quite upset. She said she had taken copious notes on the names of all my recommended flowers and scoured the flea markets for the right containers, but somehow her garden looked a mess. I went to see for myself. She was right. She had planted all of my favorite flowers in some wonderful old containers—purple echinacea, red nasturtiums, pink morning glories, scarlet runner beans, marguerite daisies, yellow and white Johnny-jump-ups, fuchsia dahlias, blue lobelia, and white roses. The result was a jumbled mess of too many colors, with no areas of focus and calming beauty. I asked if she had skipped my class on color and she

**A tight color palette of
both pinks and yellows,**
OPPOSITE, **makes graceful
potted garden combina-
tions with petunias and
yarrow,** ABOVE LEFT, **zinnias,** ABOVE RIGHT, **ranunculus,** BELOW LEFT, **and
cosmos,** BELOW RIGHT. **A
vivid red pepper empha-
sizes the color of its
slightly riper purple
neighbor,** RIGHT.

said she didn't remember any class on color.

To save the garden in a hurry, we sacrificed a few plants. Most of the flowers were in the purple and yellow range. We pulled all the reds and the reddest shades of orange, and moved some of the purple flowers around so that there would be larger chunks of similar color together. The result was a cohesive, natural-looking garden. No one dahlia stole the show, and the garden was at peace with itself and its gardener.

Remember, too, that the hues of each color are as important as the color itself. The sunnier the garden is or the farther south it is, the brighter the color and hues need to be. A red found in nature in Maine is barely related to a red growing naturally in New Mexico; the red of a hibiscus is much brighter than the leaf of a Japanese maple tree. If you want a colorful garden, there are endless shades of the same color to provide variety and depth, but a garden with more than two vivid colors can look garish and unnatural.

To begin your garden design, choose one favorite color. That color will have a few ideal color complements that will work best with it. If the color is a primary one—red, yellow, or blue—choose its complementary secondary color, the one directly opposite it on the color wheel. For instance, the complement to red is green, to yellow is purple, and to blue is orange. Let these two colors dictate all the other colors and hues. For an elegant, lush feel, keep a very narrow palette of one primary color, straying only a few shade degrees in one direction or the other. For example, an all-blue garden filled with lobelia, delphiniums, and liriope will look beautiful with maroon sunflowers and purple coneflowers. And although the garden is considered a blue garden, it may actually extend from blue to purple on the red side and to aqua on the yellow (a tight range on both sides of blue).

For a bit of variation, choose up to two secondary colors that work well together on

and size in a garden as well. To make a far corner appear closer, plant light, bright colors such as white, vivid orange, and canary yellow. To make a large space cozy, move the edges in by planting light colors in far corners and darker hues closer to the seating areas. To create distance, use pastel and dark colors. For an even greater illusion of depth, use one color, placing the lighter shades nearer, fading darker at the back. Repetition of one color will always make a space appear much larger than it actually is. For variety, plant large clumps of the same color, using a wide range of plants. For example, combining purple loosestrife with echinacea, morning glories, wild lavender roses, lisianthus, campanula, blue lobelia, liriope muscari, and purple pansies will add depth, size, and a lusher, more wild feel to any tiny space.

the color wheel. Purple hyacinth planted with early-blooming 'Apricot Beauty' tulips, for instance, is a spectacular combination. Blue asters with tiny yellow Swan River daisies is breathtaking. Red roses underplanted with lavender petunias is elegant. Yellow lantana with peach yarrow looks almost edible. Peach columbine enhances purple violets. Some of my personal favorite color combinations are blue, purple, and orange; red, purple, and green; and yellow, peach, and white.

White is a bold, useful color in the garden. It can highlight a neighboring color as well as show up brilliantly at night or in dark corners. White is so striking that it can easily stand alone. An all-white garden of oxalis, ribbon grass, geraniums, tea roses, and snapdragons makes an exquisite statement.

Color can help to create the illusion of depth

Flower size is another factor to consider when thinking about color. The larger the actual blossom, the more closely colors will have to blend. One bright red peony will stand out like a sore thumb in the midst of orange daylilies. If you want a change of color throughout your garden, use flowers with

smaller blossoms to smooth out the areas of transition between colors.

Planting the same flowers in several different areas and in a number of different containers gives continuity to an otherwise eclectic design. It will also prevent any one area from stealing too much focus.

If you are fortunate enough to have a lot of sun where you garden, your color choices are abundant. Tiny gardens, patio gardens, and indoor gardens frequently suffer from a lack of light. A shade garden is a bit more challenging, but not without tremendous rewards. Foliage comes in a wide variety of colors as well. Subtle shifts in greens, browns, reds, purples, and white can be achieved without a single blossom.

With a potted garden, the color of the container is as important as that of the flower. Nothing will ruin the look of a beautiful flowering gardenia faster than housing it in an ugly pink plastic pot. Use the color of the container to enhance the plant, not to draw attention from it. It is often best to select a

container in the same tight color palette as the plants. Red peppers, for instance, look terrific planted in a red coffee tin, or purple pansies in a blue roasting pan. Natural containers are the most versatile because they will go with anything and be reminiscent of the earth. A container decorated with bold colors or a busy design is usually best suited to a monochromatic planting that matches one of the colors. Dark plants often look best paired with dark containers.

Arranging with Potted Plants

A potted garden is a miniature garden, and all the factors of design that make a full-size garden successful—height, texture, and color—need to be considered. Arranging plants for a potted garden is not unlike arranging cut flowers in a vase. Some basic rules are helpful for beginners, but remember, rules are made to

be broken. Be daring. Experiment with combinations and admit defeat if the end result doesn't look good. A beautiful flower will not focus attention away from a jarring color combination. Our eyes are equally attuned to look at what we don't like as to what we do. Combine plants that complement instead of compete with each other.

Plants with similar growing conditions will be happiest together. At the very least, they must share the same light requirements. If soil, food, and watering requirements differ, a number of different smaller containers can be placed separately into one larger container. Then to unify the garden or simply to hide the smaller containers, cover it with moss or sprawling foliage from its own or neighboring pots.

Jasmine, creeping fig, and oxalis, for example, can be planted in happy harmony because they all need plenty of sun, moist soil, and a regular feeding schedule. Kalanchoe, begonias, and ivies would not work together because they have different light requirements. Kalanchoe and creeping fig could join in a large container, but they must be planted separately because although they share the same light

needs, kalanchoe likes to dry out between waterings and the fig must be kept evenly moist. Since no one plant will bloom year-round, foliage is as important as the flowers, and every potted garden depends heavily on the placement and choice of greenery, in addition to the interest and charm of the container.

Match the most prominent plants in the potted garden with the size and shape of the container. Assess the space needs of the roots and pay attention to the overall look. A tall container usually looks best with a trailing plant combined with one that has some height. Smaller blooms and more foliage are better suited to the outer edges of a potted garden than to its center. Variegated leaves work better with solid-color blooms and containers that are not too busy. Symmetry effects a more formal feel, while variations in height and texture will look more natural and easygoing.

Before planting a potted garden, experiment with the placement by arranging the plants in their nursery pots directly in the container. Mix and match varieties of plants and colors until the combination looks right to you. Abrupt changes in height, texture, or color can look quite contrived, so work in variations of each with smooth transitions. Only by exploring numerous combinations will you come up with a truly sensational piece.

hunt

as fall descends, and ground-bound gardeners plant their bulbs and turn to their knitting to stave off depression, my spirit soars in anticipation of junk-hunting season. I pack a bag, fill the tank in my truck, and head north every weekend. The leaves in Maine and New Hampshire have turned an orange inherited from the sun, and everything feels right with the world. From Labor Day to Thanksgiving, prices at antiques stores, tag sales, and country auctions often drop in preparation for the long cold winter and long cold storage for unsold treasures. For the container gardener, it is time to clean out the attic and to take to the

An old English watering can, ABOVE, and colorfully labeled old tins, OPPOSITE, are precious finds at flea markets nowadays.

open road in search of sidewalk heirlooms and country relics.

The pleasure of potted gardening is as much in the scavenging as in the planting. I am nearly as euphoric when I find a beautiful old wooden sap bucket in a flea market as I am when the first tulip emerges in my garden each spring. Whether you start with the containers or the plants, a potted garden plan must remain flexible. The treasures you anticipate finding are rarely the ones you will ultimately end up with. It is advisable to have at least a general idea of the flowers, shrubs, and trees you plan your pots to contain before you begin to hunt, since the plants will determine the size and type of containers appropriate for your garden. But leave open the possibility for a great container to inspire a whole new garden design. Perhaps because, like living things, they show the evidence of the passage of time, the discarded and forgotten remnants of a sweeter past enhance the garden most. Use your imagination when scouring a flea market or attic. Look at an old butter churn and picture a clematis planted in its base to trellis up the stir pole. An old orange crate with the label nearly worn away might contain a miniature field of bright orange poppies next spring. An old tomato can planted with basil and oregano on a kitchen windowsill will remind you to cook Italian favorites more often.

After years of experience, I prefer the impro-

visational approach to potted garden planning. Your first efforts may not always work out, but you'll have fun trying, and most containers are inexpensive enough to justify the cost of experimentation. I look at the space the potted garden will fill, whether a room or a yard, and imagine the general look I want to achieve, be it formal or informal. If you are the organized type or you don't want to end up with anything you don't need, write down all the potential plants and seeds you plan to use before you set off to antiques country. Approximate how much growing space you will need by estimat-

The very best place to find treasures for your garden is in your own attic. Before venturing too far away or spending too much money, take a look at the remnants of your own family's past.

ing the number of plants and the root space of each choice. If you don't know, ask at your local nursery, or call the 800 numbers in plant catalogs for some help.

In general, a big plant such as a tree often requires a lot of space below. As a rule of thumb, perennials need more space than annuals, and succulents need the least of all. Vegetables can vary but typically do not need as much root space as their height and size might suggest. The size of the pot a plant is sold in at the nursery is usually a good indication of the root space required. When in doubt about the size of the container, it is better to err on the side of too much soil rather than too little. A plant placed in too small a container, however, can often survive if it is watered and fed frequently. A more drastic but effective way to keep a plant thriving in a small container is to turn out the root ball from time to time and trim back the roots with a sharp knife. This is a variation on the bonsai technique used to make miniature trees, and all plants treated in this way will remain smaller than those "potted up" to large containers.

Once you have imagined your dream container garden, tuck your list in your pocket and . . .

Hidden among the discarded typewriters, LEFT, and old milk bottles, OPPOSITE, **are pails and cans that are ideal for planting.**

Let the Hunt Begin

WARNING: The hunt can become an addiction. It is important to watch for the early signs of this malady and approach a flea market with decorum and moderation. If your heart begins to race a bit faster when you pass a sign reading TAG SALE AHEAD on a country road, you were born to create a potted garden. Lest this obsession get out of hand, learn to set limits on your acquisitions. You do not want to end up in a poorhouse full of junk. Remember, the purpose of potted gardening is to bring beauty, not clutter, into your life.

The very best treasures are always gathered from your own backyard. Gardeners who live in the country may find old box crates, rusted toys, and wooden sleds lurking in barns and garages. An old wooden ladder that might threaten a house painter's life would make a fine

The old paper press in the middle of this pile of "junk," RIGHT, **would make an ideal planter for a large potted tree. The door could be opened in a few years, in order to trim the roots to contain the growth.**

RIGHT: **At an auction in New Hampshire, sap buckets are sold in bulk to the highest bidder. On this day, I was the only bidder!**

trellis for morning glories, and an old cattle feeding trough that served its last meal a century ago could now serve as a raised vegetable garden. The suburbs may yield the old tin milk containers that sat on the doorstep of every home in the 1960s or the battered toolbox in the basement or garage. But no habitat affords as much discarded junk for the potted

OPPOSITE: **Glass bottles,** ABOVE LEFT, **make ideal vases for cut flowers. Nineteenth-century and early 20th-century dough boxes, wooden trunks, bait cans, English washtubs, and galvanized pails can still be gathered up in bulk at country auctions and flea markets. City markets usually garner a much higher price, as each piece is sold separately.**

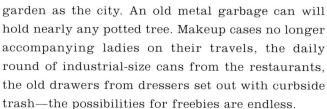

garden as the city. An old metal garbage can will hold nearly any potted tree. Makeup cases no longer accompanying ladies on their travels, the daily round of industrial-size cans from the restaurants, the old drawers from dressers set out with curbside trash—the possibilities for freebies are endless.

Beauty Is in the Eye of the Beholder

The criteria for a good container are simple: Are the shape, color, and texture appealing to you? Is it sturdy? Will it hold a plant of any size? Will it last longer than a week? The piece should have a practical, natural opening in the top so that soil and plants

**Don't forget your tetanus
shots before venturing
into a dump site,** OPPOSITE,
**and pass by the old gas
cans; they can never be
cleaned well enough and
will kill the plants you try
to grow in them. Antiques
stores in small towns or
on back roads are full of
possibilities,** LEFT.
**When even the front
porch is cluttered with
containers, the store is
probably a mecca for the
potted garden.**

can be placed inside. The bottom should be flat
enough to allow the container to stand on its own (if
not, it can still be used as a hanging planter). If
there are no natural drainage holes in the piece,
there must be a way to drill them in it without
breaking the piece or your tools. If there are too
many holes, as in a colander or a dryer drum, there
must be an attractive way of filling enough of them
so that the soil does not wash away. Even if a container does not meet all of these criteria, it may still
find a place in the garden as an ornamental accent.

If you love it, take it
home; you can figure out
what to do with it later.

   The warmth and nat-
ural texture of a wooden
box or barrel make it a
magnificent earthy con-
tainer for any plant. The
older the box, the more
likely it is that it was con-
structed with dovetailed
joints. Before the advent

**If you love it and you
don't know what it is,
take it home and figure
out what to do with it
later,** RIGHT. **The best
garden ornaments are
often those salvaged
from another architec-
tural role.**

of screws, the sides of a box (or of a piece of furniture, for that matter) were secured with tongue and groove joints. This dovetailing makes the piece more valuable, but it also makes it more likely to pull apart when moisture causes the joints to expand and warp. The seams can be reinforced with a simple nail, but bear in mind that dovetailed boxes still won't last as long as a box held together with brackets and screws. Nevertheless, the great thing about using wood to hold plants is that it lets the soil breathe much like terra cotta does. Air is as important to a plant as water and sun are.

Glass can be a tricky medium to plant in because it is clear and breakable. If a glass container doesn't already have a hole, forget about trying to drill one—it will crack. Glass can be

used for a temporary, indoor potted garden. It is perfect for paperwhite narcissus bulbs that will grow in just water and rocks. Beautiful old glass bottles make wonderful cut-flower vases.

Copper washtubs and buckets make lovely planters, although copper compounds will leach into the soil and can significantly alter its chemical composition. Line all copper containers with extra-heavy-duty garbage bags to prevent any unwanted soil changes.

Any piece that tells a story will add additional charm to your home or garden. Old English washtubs with hand-pounded grooves to ease in the hand-washing of clothes are wonderful reminders of a far more difficult, if simpler, life. An old metal mailbox with the name of the owner of the house in 1839 makes the perfect memorial garden. Canadian sap buckets, color coded to remind the Smiths that sap collected in the red bucket belongs to the Joneses, and the pink, vice versa. Containers rich in history and lore elevate the beauty of any garden tenfold.

My aunt Timmy gave me the potbelly stove

Pile up a number of items before you start negotiating for a better price. The more you buy, the more willing the dealer is to deal.

from my great-grandmother's home. It has a place of honor in front of the mantel in my living room. Over the holes that once heated my ancestors' meals rest two cast-iron pots spilling ivy and creeping fig. I think of my great-grandmother often.

Where to Look

The hunt has as many destinations as there are containers. Once you begin to look with a hunter's eyes, every place people might leave or sell the containers of yesterday is a good place to go. Be careful not to trespass when scavenging or to remove what belongs to someone else. Other than that, the following are great sources for that ultimate "find."

Your own backyard likely holds the greatest treasures of your family history and way of life. Scour the garage, conquer the attic, and tear open the closet. You are sure to find something—old motor-oil cans, hatboxes, or sweater drawers—to plant in. Much of my own garden is contained in sidewalk heirlooms, scavenged right from the streets of New York.

Flea markets can be an endless source of discarded heirlooms for gardening. The best containers may be found under the tables—the boxes that carried the junk to market. Most major cities have an open-air flea market once a week in good weather.

Local newspapers advertise them regularly. The prices of most flea-market items are flexible, so don't hesitate to negotiate.

Antiques stores have a wealth of good stuff, but most shop owners have gone to the same flea markets or auctions as you. They just showed up earlier and bought more, and now need to get top dollar for their effort. It would be easy to break your bank if you bought all your garden treasures from an antiques store, so buy only the unique, one-of-a-kind things you just won't find anywhere else. It is also a good idea to make friends with the owners and dealers that carry the sort of things you like. Let them know what you are looking for and they may call you when they find little gems up your alley. Steer away from very expensive antiques that will break or ruin easily.

Dump picking is my personal favorite way to shop. My aunt and uncle live in a small New

England town with the typical town dump. Every time I visit, we head for the dump, armed with the proper sticker on the car windshield, for an afternoon of great adventure. We are greeted enthusiastically by the dump director, who won a million dollars from a magazine sweepstakes a couple of years ago but loves her job too much to ever quit. If she knows I'm coming, she will have a pile of rusty detergent tins and old milk crates awaiting my arrival. We make for the metal heap and carefully dig in. This is not a job for the fainthearted, for there are certainly dangers in dump picking. Since the chances of getting a rusty cut are rather high, a recent tetanus shot is a must.

Tag and barn sales are terrific hunting grounds for containers as well as for garden furniture. Generally, things are cheap, cheap, cheap. It is usually best to go early to get the pick of the lot, although you may pay a bit more. If you arrive late in the day, you may still discover items left by the typical shopper that are just the treasures you need—boxes, barrels, and wonderful rusty things.

On the way to dinner with friends

one evening, I found a discarded

enamel kitchen sink awaiting an early-morning garbage pickup. My friends begged and

pleaded with me to leave it until after dinner, suggesting that no one on earth (but me,

obviously) would want this piece of junk. My head knew they were wrong, but my heart

leaned toward dinner with my friends. Dinner was divine, but the sink meanwhile was

scavenged by a kindred soul. A year later I

found another sink on the sidewalk and, with

help, carried it right home to my garden. It

now sits planted on my terrace with

columbines, ivy, and violets.

The adventure of finding great planters can

bring as much joy as gardening. But there

are some keys to successful hunting.

the game

NO DUMP PICKING
IF YOU SEE SOMETHING YOU WANT, PLEASE ASK ATTENDANT

1 When leisurely traveling from one spot to the next, look for the route that bypasses interstates and major highways. The chances of finding an antiques shop or a tag sale increase with the view. The problem, of course, is that if you do have a destination, you may never arrive.

2 Have some idea of what you are looking for—a style, a look, a size, a solution to a particular growing or space problem. It's dangerous to shop with absolutely nothing in mind; you could end up with nothing you need.

3 Buy only what you can use *this year.*

4 Look for design and practicality in the same object. If the piece contains only one of these elements, leave it behind.

5 Don't ever spend more than your instinct tells you the item is worth.

6 Don't buy expensive antiques to garden in. The elements will be even harsher than the price.

7 Look through the whole market, shop, or tag sale before buying. Then go back to the things you remember liking. If the containers still move you, consider buying half of them. Anything that has disappeared by the time you return was never destined for your garden.

8 Always ask courteously if the seller could give you a better price. Most dealers of secondhand and antique merchandise will take 10 percent off the asking price, if you ask nicely. Some will even give a bigger discount if you buy a lot and/or pay cash. Some dealers won't, so don't haggle. Hunting for garden containers and accessories should be fun, not stressful. Walk away if you don't like the price or the seller. The pleasure of collecting old stuff is the story behind the piece, and if the memory of buying it is unpleasant, the piece will never make you happy.

For the average container gardener, these rules should be sufficient to help you accumulate the needed materials for any size garden. But if you are anything like me, with a chronic addiction to shopping and junk, you may need to set some more advanced restrictions on your happy hunting. In order to keep my family, my friends, and my sanity, I have set some advanced rules for junkaholics.

9 Stop only if you see a sign enough in advance to turn off the road safely without turning around. If you pass it, let it go; it wasn't meant to be.

10 Don't change your route for a sign. Following an arrow off your original route can cause enough stress to actually end a long relationship. No butter churn or galvanized tub is worth that. Don't learn the hard way. If you don't think you can follow rule ten, let someone else drive through particularly tempting territory to protect you from yourself.

gather

K nowing the Latin name of every plant indigenous to your zone can be helpful and certainly impressive, but it's not necessary to your growing efforts. I retain Latin plant names like I retain jokes: in one ear and out the other. And although I am not proud of my lack of horticultural retention, I no longer allow it to intimidate my choices or questions at a nursery. You'll find, actually, that most horticulturists are quite pleased to know more than you do. Never hesitate to ask what you do not know. And once you know enough to feel confident, remember to share your knowledge with the neophyte potted gardener.

At a nursery I am like a kid in a candy store, OPPOSITE. ABOVE: **Violas will bloom from spring into fall if diligently deadheaded and planted in partial shade.**

I usually overbuy both plants and containers hoping there will be a little space off in the corner where I can tuck a little something in. Leftovers find their way to happy friends' gardens.

A Basic Plan

My refrigerator is always empty. I suppose after 12 years in New York City I have developed the native ritual of shopping for every meal separately. To make matters worse, I usually find myself in the middle of a ridiculously crowded aisle, wild from hunger, grabbing anything in sight. No plan, no recipe, no idea what I want for dinner. I become overwhelmed, cranky, and spendthrift. I arrive home, broke and starving, only to discover I have bought nothing but cookies, cheese, milk, coffee, soda, and soap.

Shopping for plants without a vague idea of the garden you want will yield the same disastrous results. Be sure to know the following about your potted garden before venturing out to a nursery. To choose the proper plants for your potted garden, think about the elements of the garden space and relate them to nature. Gardeners planning a sunny patio planting in Phoenix, Arizona, should look to the desert for inspiration. A potted garden for a porch in Minnesota shaded by a 50-year-old oak is best modeled after the woodlands, with their range of ferns and flowering plants that thrive under the same conditions. If you live atop a high-rise in Boston, look to the White Mountains, where birch and juniper predominate.

Michael Trapp elongates geraniums, adding extraordinary drama, OPPOSITE, to an otherwise ordinary plant. Lemon thyme sprawls out of the head of Prince Albert, LEFT, needing water twice a day.

Indoor Plants

Most nongardeners who come into my shop looking for an indoor plant want one that will flower year-round with little or no sunlight. There is not a plant in the world that can satisfy that request. I gently steer them toward a choice of beautiful textured foliage of a Rex begonia, maidenhair fern, or variegated ivy. Once we add a few forced bulbs to their potted garden for a splash of temporary color, they are pleased. It warms my heart when some return three weeks later to find another blooming plant to replace the dead tulips. Most are hooked—a gardener is born.

Imagine an indoor potted garden as a miniature garden, complete with trees, ground cover, and a splash of color. When choosing a variety of plants that need the same amount of sunlight, also consider how well they will do without much air circulation and with

Is it a cat or catmint (Nepeta) that awakens Big Red, RIGHT? The basket and basket chair share a common origin.

constant warm temperatures. All plants need some amount of air circulation, but some are particularly sensitive and succumb to mildew when grown indoors. Remember, too, that a plant that has spent its entire life in a greenhouse, under ideal growing conditions, will have a hard time adjusting to ideal human living conditions. Most flowering annuals will look unhappy after a week or so. Alpines and other winter-hardy plants need a cold spell to thrive. And, although they often look out of place up north, tropical plants have become an office staple because they like the steady warm temperature day in and day out and because many can survive neglect.

Some potted gardens in an office or apartment building with central heat and air and no windows that can be opened may have to be considered temporary. Bulbs, azaleas, poinsettias, begonias, kalanchoe, primroses, and African violets are all fairly long-lasting under these conditions, but none looks good forever. Many nonflowering plants such as ivy and ficus thrive indoors. Fans can help increase the survival rate in these tight spaces.

One way to extend the life of the indoor potted garden is to choose two or three indoor-hardy, easy-to-grow green plants such as ivy and ferns and include just one or two blooming plants. When the blooms wither on the flowering plant, simply cut back the flower stems to the hardiest leaves, or remove the plant altogether by digging up the bulb or root ball. Let the greens fill in the hole left, or replace one blooming specimen with another. Depending on the type of flowering plant that was removed, you may want to transplant the root ball or bulb outdoors, give it to a nurturing friend, or simply toss it.

Some of my favorite nonflowering indoor plants are:

- Creeping ficus (adorable leaves and not too finicky)
- Ivy (fairly easy, sometimes buggy, and often overwatered)
- Many fabulous ferns (which need to be watered often)
- Most of the succulent family (neglect makes them grow even better)
- Rex begonia (beautiful varied leaves, easy to grow)
- Caladium (wonderful colored leaves)

Rosemary, ivy, and gloxinia climb a ladder of successful indoor plants, OPPOSITE. **Oxalis in a "piss pot" flowers continually when watered and fed often on this sunny windowsill,** RIGHT.

Some of my favorite flowering plants are:

- Oxalis (great leaves, grows like a weed; purple is my favorite)
- African violets (not as difficult as their reputation, but not so attractive when not in bloom)
- Orchids (can be expensive, but the flower lasts a very long time)
- Miniature roses (nearly impossible to keep bug free and alive for any length of time indoors; think of them as long-lasting cut flowers)
- All bulbs (short lived, but quite showy)
- Azaleas (the bloom lasts forever)
- Gerbera daisy (big colorful flowers, but a bit fussy about watering)
- Wedding veil (great filler with little white flowers)
- Bacopa (tiny flowers, cute little leaves; can get scraggly after a while)
- Begonias (spectacular flowers, great leaves; need diligent cutting back)
- Primroses (what a flower—no wonder they need so much attention)
- Poinsettias (a real winter treat, especially the peach and white)
- Kalanchoe (vivid tiny bunches of flowers; sun and neglect; looks dreary when not blooming)
- Cyclamen (flowers and leaves are exquisite; does not like to be transplanted; keep cool)
- Hydrangea (the beauty lasts only a few weeks, but well worth it)
- Grasses (often overlooked in container gardening, but can add the most graceful, moving, and dramatic textures and shapes to any garden; most require a lot of sun to do well, but several can tolerate partial shade; the best thing about grasses in containers is that, like the crushes of our youth, the more they are neglected, the more they'll thrive)

There are hundreds more plants to grow indoors, so scour greenhouses for surprises.

Where Are All the Flowers Grown

Although catalogs are an endless source of entertainment and distraction during the long winter months, they are not always the best sources for container gardening, both indoors and out. Conditions in a container are rarely as ideal as in the ground. Well-established roots living in soil are needed to ensure a healthy, long life in captivity. When ordering perennials and tubers from a catalog, note how the plants will arrive. Because of the difficulty in mailing live plants, many roots and tubers will arrive in a dormant, bare-root state. Although this is a cheaper and perfectly fine method for shipping plants that will be grown in the ground, container plants will do best if they arrive already potted in soil. Many catalogs indicate the size of the container in which such plants are shipped. In general, the larger the container,

the better. For container gardening, local nurseries and farmers' markets are by far the best places for inspiration, education, and product. Although not every nursery is stocked with the most exotic new plants, you will not only be able to choose healthy, growing plants by looking at them, you also can ask questions about each and learn if they do well in your area. In addition, nurseries can supply flats of many annuals already started. This is helpful for the container gardener who has a shorter growing season or lack of space to sow seeds indoors.

A basic knowledge of the location, temperature, and hazards of your own gardening space is a must. How much sun will the garden get? Take notes on the hour the sun reaches a certain area and when it leaves. Keep in mind that the position of the sun will shift dramatically from winter to spring. A sunny spot in January may be shady by July, particularly if large trees or tall buildings are nearby. The advantage of potted gardening is that if you make an error in your calculations, you can shift the containers to a more ideal spot. But since you won't want to move everything, don't overbuy, and select plants that can do well in

part sun and part shade, such as nicotiana, lobelia, dianthus, and campanula. After a full year of observation, you can be more specific about your plant choices, adding full-sun and full-shade plants as needed.

Learn what temperature zone you live in and how cold your winters are. Then figure out which areas of your garden may vary from your designated zone. When a garden is on a rooftop or an exposed terrace or deck high above the ground, it could get 10° to 20° F hotter in the summer and the same amount colder in the winter. If there are no walls or trees protecting some areas, they may be battered by strong winds. On the other hand, if there is a lot of protection from the wind on all sides, the garden may stay much warmer in the winter than the zone map predicts. Even within the garden, microclimates may exist. One spot could be very dark, windy, and cold and another quite sunny, warm, and sheltered. Each one of these conditions will warrant different plant selections, so the key is to get a feeling for the location at different times of the day and in different seasons of the year before buying your plants.

Perhaps the least asked but most important question for anyone planning a garden is, how much work does the gardener want to do? The answer to

that question will determine how much to buy as well as what to buy. Some plants require very little care and others need daily attention all year long. If you do not plan to install an automatic watering system, all container gardens need frequent waterings. If you know you will not water every day, choose only drought-resistant plants such as reed grass, yarrow, and gazania and very large containers that will hold water longer.

Do you want your garden to look good all year round with only one planting? If you live in a warm climate, your biggest issue will be selecting plants that will survive the relentless heat of the summer. If your area freezes in the winter, direct your attention to evergreens and winter-flowering perennials. Because space is so limited in container gardening, you will have to sacrifice a great deal of color if you do not want to replant twice a year.

Cost is another crucial factor in the selection, size, and quantity of plants. Perennials are more expensive than annuals, but they will last, on average, about three years in a container; an annual, as its name implies, lasts merely one where there is a winter freeze. Trees and shrubs are usually the biggest expense, but you can save money by buying a younger tree and having the pleasure of watching it grow to the ideal size. Set a budget for yourself and then divide it between plants and containers. At first, about half of your budget may have to go to your containers, unless you a very good scavenger and you give yourself enough time to hunt. Those lucky enough to have containers from previous years still need to plan for additional containers for specific plants and replacements for those that do not survive the winter. With the remainder of your funds, try to spend only one-half to two-thirds on plants on your first trip to the nursery. There will always be more you will want or need, so it's good to have a little reserve. Once armed with all the necessary information and questions, as well as a basic idea of what you want your garden

Nurseries that grow their own plants from their own healthy stock are incredible resources for both plants and knowledge, OPPOSITE AND RIGHT. **Peek into the greenhouses that are off limits to the public. If the plants look good and the benches are tidy, buy with confidence.**

to look like, head for your local nursery with an open mind.

Select a nursery that grows its own plants from its own healthy stock. This way you can be assured that the roots are well established and that the plant is adaptable to your climate. Look for a nursery that has greenhouses with young plants not yet for sale and sections of fully grown plants (or stock) also not for sale. This is the sure sign they grow their own plants. As tempting as the lower prices at some large hardware and retail chains are, try to resist buying from them. The longevity and health of your plant may be at stake. But even more important, independently owned nurseries and independent growers, using their own stock and educating a new generation of gardeners, are a dying breed. It is crucial that we treasure them and do nothing to hasten their demise.

In 1986, I was working for the National AIDS Hotline in New York City. To calm myself from the stress of the job, every day for lunch I would wander through the farmers' market in the city's Union Square. Over a hundred farmers trucked in their vegetables, flowers, and fresh-baked pies from hundreds of miles away to sell to the city dwellers. When the hotline finally became too much for me, I began working for some of the farmers selling flowers, cut and potted.

One family came from five generations of poultry and livestock farming. By the early 1980s they were the last of their neighbors to still own their farm. Facing bankruptcy, they called a family meeting and agreed to try anything to save it. Flowers seemed to be selling in the city, so they converted their chicken coops into greenhouses and began growing annuals. The business took off. Ten years later, they are not just surviving but have expanded the farm, and they are now selling a large number of perennials as well. They specialize in flowering plants that grow well in containers for the typical city gardener.

Half of my garden was dug up from a field and left unweeded and wild in rusty, dented cans. The sunflowers in my garden were all sown by the birds who enjoy their meal underneath the feeders I fill daily.

I think of them every time I am tempted to purchase a really cheap plant from a big retail chain. The satisfaction of knowing that my city garden is helping to sustain a sixth generation of farmers three hours from the city is worth the extra few cents.

Sowing Seeds

When another farmer friend of mine lost her rented farm a few years back, she moved to the city to start a very different life. She had no trouble finding friends and work, but plenty finding sun. Her tiny apartment had only one window facing north. But, as every farmer knows, spring is only spring when the seedlings sprout. She rigged a multimirror contraption around her entire living room to reflect the sun from the windows across the street. On her window ledge, she stacked five layers of seed starters and sowed a huge variety of seeds. Scarcely a dozen little flowers or vegetables actually yielded blossoms from the thousands of seeds carefully tended twice daily for six weeks. A thermometer guided the plastic wrap, on or off, to either prevent mildew or retain moisture. She watered daily and blow-dried weekly in a ritual unfamiliar to us city folk. That spring I visited the farmers' market and nurseries with a new

Grasses, weeds, scaveola, roses, and zinnias create a harmonious wild mix on my own rooftop garden.

admiration for the growers of all those perfect little plants.

For the city and container gardener looking for the thrill of growing from seed, but without my farmer friend's perseverance, simply throw easy-to-grow morning glory and scarlet runner bean seeds directly into your pots outdoors in the spring. By the time you have completely forgotten about them, little surprises will pop up all over your garden. You can proudly tell all your friends when they visit your garden, "I grew these from seed." They will be most impressed.

When planting seeds directly into a pot, read the package directions carefully. Many seeds will germinate more readily when soaked for 24 hours before planting. Some like to be nicked with a knife to break their natural coating. Sow more seeds than is recommended on the package. You can always thin the seedlings later if all survive.

A Weed Is a Flower Looking for a Good Home

In my little shop in Greenwich Village, I wile away the hours happily making quirky little bunches of cut-flower arrangements to sell to the many curiosity seekers who come in "just looking." Susie, who works with me, grew up in her mother's beautiful flower shop in southern Delaware and knows far more about cut flowers and traditional arranging than I do. We share many of the duties of the flower shop, the most important being buying the cut flowers from the wholesale market. I am always struck by the different choices she and I make. She laughs when I come in with two large bundles of my version of the crème de la crème of the early-morning pick. "Weeds," she says with a wry smile. I puff up defensively and reply each time, "They are not weeds; they're just not what your mother taught you to buy."

I love a wild look. I love flowers that look as though they were plucked from a meadow a moment ago. I love grasses and reeds and pale, odd shapes. I love flowers half spent, petals

Loosestrife is one of the few plants I encourage pulling up. It looks great and causes no damage to the environment contained in a pot, whereas it will cause plenty if left to continue to clog this Connecticut waterway.

falling off, overripe, underpicked. I suppose it's the journey, the story, the nature I love. For me, perfection is too hard to look at. The untamed flourish of loosestrife, echinacea, reed grass, and creeping thyme battling each other for space in a whiskey barrel is an exquisite attempt to contain nature.

The least expensive way to accumulate plants is to receive them from friends or to gather them from nature. The latter is very tricky. Always check with your state and local environmental groups before digging up any plant not on your own property. Many plants are protected by law and should not be touched.

Some plants truly are considered weeds. Purple loosestrife, for instance, has become so insidious in Connecticut, where it has clogged the waterways and threatens native species, that it can no longer be legally sold in nurseries there. Although it would not be advisable to plant loosestrife in the ground where it can spread, contained in a pot it is a joy. I love to dig up clumps of it every time I need a tall plant in a pot that does not drain well. It is the perfect plant for a swampy pot garden!

realize

m y first garden as an adult was a tiny herb garden planted in a cookie tin sent by my grand- mother to me in college. Although it was small and rather hardy, it was plenty to handle. I was barely able to take care of myself at 18, let alone anything else. Miraculously, that herb garden sup- plied my dormitory with fresh thyme and rosemary for the gourmet touch to an endless supply of instant chicken noodle soup and macaroni and powdered cheese. My little gar- den in turn inspired a friend down the hall to grow tomatoes in her elec- tric curler cover. Although tomatoes

Tonka garden, ABOVE, dumps the plas- tic pot idea. Hybrid "Susies" nes- tled, RIGHT, are in a suitcase lined with foil and topped with moss. Russian sage (Perovskia), PREVIOUS PAGES, is buggy bound.

never appeared, the tiny farm provided fodder for politically volatile agricultural discussions, as well as acres of laughter. Tomatoes were not really the point.

Instead of bringing Mom a bouquet of flowers next Mother's Day, give her the whole garden! Plant some ivy in an old birdhouse and thank her for helping you fly the coop. Rather than having another bake sale to raise the money for a new playground, auction off herbs in tin cans and flowers in an old toy truck. Considering the cost of flowers for a wedding, imagine how much greater the effect would be if the centerpieces became the newlyweds' first garden.

Today we have as little connection to the cut-flower growers as we do to the "farmer" providing our milk. Sadly, many cut-flower farms have gone the way of dairy farms. Small family-owned businesses have been replaced by massive corporate plantations. Flowers and cows are bred to produce more, longer, better, with terrible chemicals that wreak unknown havoc on the laborers and the land.

A child who learns to nurture a little plant on her bedroom windowsill may one day care for her own magnificent garden. The city dweller and condo owner need not deprive themselves of the joys of gardening. The possibilities are endless.

Urns need not always be planted symmetrically. The allium, monarda, potato vine mix, BELOW, is an elegant variation. Coreopsis Sunray, viola, and gazania dance in and around an old CHARMS can, OPPOSITE.

Outdoors

The most attractive and successful potted gardens are those that nearly meld with the scenery around them. Containers can be used to add focus and drama to naturally beautiful landscapes. Steps and doors can be accented with interesting textures of both containers and plants. Expansive backyards can feel cozier when potted gardens line the property. Formality and symmetry go hand in hand with similar containers planted all in a row.

Pots in the Garden

When my friend Nicole volunteered to plant a garden in the 20-by-10-foot space behind her high-rise apartment in New York City, she began by buying a couple hundred dollars' worth of plants at the farmers' market. She consulted with me on additives for the soil and ways to transplant the ivy that had taken over the whole backyard. She had asked her co-op board to give her some money to offset the cost of the garden, and they obliged with a tenth of what she had asked for. Two weeks into the project my friend called me in a panic. She said she had ruined the backyard, had spent all her money, was going to have to move out, and promised to give up gardening forever. I rushed over to assess the damage for myself. She was right; it looked a lot worse than when she began. But I knew it would take only a bit of ingenuity and very little money to make it beautiful.

The plot of land consisted of one large elm tree nestled on a small hill, with concrete surrounding three sides and an old wooden fence protecting the alley next door. The tree and the buildings blocked most of the light. The soil was poor and rocky. The amount of money and labor it would take to make this little plot a viable perennial garden was enormous. I assured Nicole that she had done as much as she could alone, and with the little money she had.

Together we replaced some, not all, of the ivy ground cover. This fashion-designer-

Old Flemish terra-cotta pots and architectural columns add drama and design to Michael Trapp's magical garden in ways that a planted border could never achieve.

turned-gardener had a penchant for old distressed iron pieces, a wonderful assortment of which were strewn about the yard. So we strategically placed the pieces in the ivy patches and filled some old pots with rich fluffy soil and shade-loving flowering plants. Each container was then positioned to highlight an architectural piece. The result of two hours of work and less than $50 more was a fantastic New York City objets d'art garden.

A Window of Opportunity

For most container gardeners, the windowsill is the most natural first step. The pleasure of a window box can be enjoyed from both the inside and the outside. It can be transplanted from season to season rather inexpensively and often watered from the comfort of indoors.

But a window box need not be just a box in a window. The entire expanse of a windowsill should be taken into account and considered a potential window garden. There is no need to mimic the shape and size of the sill with your window garden. Frequently, the strongest element of any design is the use of free space. In other words, position a minigarden at the far end of a windowsill and leave the rest of the ledge clear and uncluttered. Oilcans and old boots can add

that fits the exact measurements of the store-bought brackets. All of the elements can be purchased individually at a hardware store as well.

Fill a window box to the brim with plants. Do not, however, start tender young plants in a window garden. If you want to grow your plants from seeds or seedlings, start them elsewhere, then transplant them when they are nearly lush and full. There is just not enough room or time to wait. Place all plants very close together, forcing them to spill over the edges.

a bit of personality to your window on the world. Conversely, if you want to cover your entire sill with a garden, an old wooden or metal toolbox is similar to the traditional window box in shape but has the added charm of something old. Some may even have a handle to trellis some jasmine or sweet pea. Chicken, horse, and goat feeders commonly have a built-in hanging device that makes their transition to a window garden almost flawless.

Most window boxes placed on an outside ledge need to be secured to prevent the container from falling. A large container can be weighed down with rocks. Manufactured devices for anchoring window boxes are sold in most nurseries. Although they are recommended for a standard terra-cotta or wooden rectangular box, most brackets are adaptable. Or simply look for an interesting container

As you select your plants, remember that a tight color palette can add size and depth to a small space. Choose flowers and foliage that work well together. Complement the container and its surrounding walls and frame with the color and texture of the plants.

Annuals are usually the best bet for a window box because they bloom from spring through fall. Perennials, on the other hand, often flower for only two or three weeks a year and need more root space than annuals. With such a tiny space, it would be a shame to waste

a moment of it out of bloom, so use perennials sparingly.

Trailing plants such as ivy or creeping fig work well in the window, and even some plants that are considered ground covers will act as trailing plants when they want to keep growing and there is no ground to cover. Ajuga is one of my favorites because the foliage is colorful, it thrives in the shade, and it has tiny little spiky blossoms in the spring. Avoid vinca, the most common trailing plant for containers. It is too long and oddly uniform in its trailing habits, not nearly as appealing as a plant that winds and bends, such as ivy or morning glories.

A terrific flowering trailing plant for window boxes is lobelia, which bears delicate little flowers in beautiful shades of purple, blue, lavender, or white. On a sunnier windowsill, nasturtiums are a perfect choice for their brilliant shades of orange, yellow, peach, and scarlet. They are quick starters and rapid growers

—the exception to the do-not-grow-from-seed rule. The leaves are a spectacular emerald green in the shape of a silver dollar. There are two different types of nasturtiums, the trailing variety and the bush variety. Combining the two is a great way to add depth while trailing.

If the window is your only garden space, you may want to plant a small tree with some smaller flowering perennials and a few annuals in a random manner. A tree will impart a sense of fullness and depth. Symmetry will add formality. In a large window box, plant about one-third of the garden with permanent trailing greens such as English ivy and evergreen trees such as junipers or boxwood. There are dozens of fantastic compact juniper varieties that grow well in the dwarfed environment of a window garden. Some will cascade down the edge of a planter.

The window is the perfect place to perch and to watch the seasons change. An empty window box for a period of time is not a very attractive sight, so remember that in the winter you should either replant all the annuals with some long-lasting perennials or simply remove the annuals and allow the English ivy to grow. Keep in mind that although evergreens stay green in the fall and winter, they often do not grow much. Thus a hole in the fall garden will still be a hole in the spring.

One of my favorite combinations in a window box is petunias and ivy. As the petunias begin to fade in fall, just pull them out and the ivy will cover most of the bare spots for the entire winter, provided you've placed the ivy plants close enough together in the spring.

Some folks like to take a break from gardening in the winter by wiring a decorative arrangement of cut evergreen berry branches and pinecones in their window container.

Watering becomes even more crucial in window gardens, because they are normally shallow and therefore drain very quickly. When a garden is planted on the inside of the window, the glass can magnify the harsh sun, causing foliage to burn and creating droughtlike conditions. Water more often, and shade the window during the most direct sun midday with an opaque material.

Water Gardens

In my early twenties, I lived on the shore of Lake Michigan on the north side of Chicago. My apartment was small, old, and rundown. The original windows were no match for the severe winds that ripped through my living room. I was chilled to the bone year in and year out, yet I could not bring myself to move. Even in the worst storm, my soul was comforted by the magnificent view of the ferocious waters. The beauty and peace that that lake brought to my life is something I will always remember.

Water is so mesmerizing it is hard to compete with. When gardening in or around water, less is more. An overly planted perennial garden surrounding a pool or near a pond can look out of place or worse, and all that work is often completely overlooked. Simple, stark lines that can be reflected clearly in the water are often best. Never block the view of the water with plants that are too loud, too dense, or too tall.

Planting a potted water garden can be rather simple. Many water plants do well in any old container, even without a pump. Some need a simple water pump to keep the water flowing. A diligent check of the water level and some plant food is about all the care most potted water gardens need.

plant

a couple of years ago, an advertising company called me out of the blue on a Tuesday afternoon to ask how much it would cost for them to make a garden on their 300-square-foot deck. I explained that I would have to come over and see the space and discuss with them what they envisioned and how it would be used and cared for. The gentleman replied, "There's no time for all that. We need a full garden by tomorrow." They were having a party for their new client, The New York Botanical Garden!

I said forget it. But much pleading, deep pockets, and the absurdity of it all charmed me into an attempt. We dragged dozens of odds and ends out of storage,

Canadian maple syrup cans await planting in the store, OPPOSITE. **Seed pots made from newspaper, ABOVE, make for simple, clean transplanting.**

Fire buckets, oilcans, and
tire wells make inexpensive,
earthy containers, BELOW.
All you need is a good potting soil and drainage holes.
If your container garden is
planted at ground level and
will not be moved, standard
potting soil should be fine,
OPPOSITE.

had a ton of soil delivered to the site, and cleared out all the local nurseries on the way to the job. It drizzled all day as we pickaxed holes in the makeshift containers, dumped in soil, and threw in the plants. And voilà! At 5:00, the sun came out, the terrace was hosed down, and the garden looked as if it had been there for years.

While I will never again attempt such folly, I tell the story as inspiration. As you look out your window at the concrete slab, wishing for a wild English garden, take heart—it is possible. Think of yourself as a painter, and the concrete as the canvas. Mix the paint and begin creating.

Mixing the Soil

The soil for a potted garden should vary in composition depending on the plants grown and the garden's location. The pH level of a soil is a scientific measure of its acidity or alkalinity. The pH scale ranges from 1 to 14, with 7 defining a neutral soil. Most plants will thrive with a pH of 5.5 to 6.5, which is a slightly acid soil. For this pH, my standard mix is equal

parts peat moss; vermiculite, perlite, or sand for good drainage; manure for nutrients; and topsoil. Woodland plants like the soil to be a bit more acidic, or "sour." To increase acidity, add more peat moss, or even coffee or tea grounds.

Succulents, some vegetables, herbs, and green grass lawns like to be in "sweeter," or more alkaline, soil. Simple, inexpensive test kits for measuring soil pH are sold in many garden and pet stores.

Since container gardeners are notoriously limited in space and sometimes in time and energy, you may wish to purchase a light, well-mixed potting soil for your potted garden. To determine how much you will need, estimate the cubic feet of all your containers, then add 10 percent more. Always buy more than you think you'll need, since soil mix is measured in a dry state—once you water your containers, the soil will settle and more will have to be added. Larger quantities of soil products are often sold by the cubic foot instead of in smaller bags, which are sold by weight. If your local nursery or garden center only has bags by weight, they will usually have a formula to estimate the cubic feet of each bag

Creeping fig, OPPOSITE, will cover the tricycle and the wall if left unchecked! Hens and chicks find a happy home in the shallow soil of an old cigar box, LEFT.

of soil mix they carry. Ask them to help you translate the weight into volume.

For a rooftop or deck garden, the soil should also be light. The heaviest ingredients in any soil mix are the topsoil and sand. To lighten the load, use only 10 percent topsoil, 30 percent vermiculite, 30 percent peat moss, and 30 percent dehydrated cow manure. Both vermiculite and perlite are good for drainage, but the former retains water better, which is important in the heat of the summer.

To save some time and energy, mix all the soil you will need in one large space rather than mixing the ingredients into each separate container. If it is not too windy and there is no chance of rain falling before you've filled all your containers, spread out a heavy plastic tarp and dump all the measured ingredients onto the center. With a shovel, mix in all the ingredients. The mix should be

Unless you are Hercules, don't forget to move heavy pots like these, RIGHT, into place before filling them with soil.

No new drainage hole is needed, RIGHT, **as this funnel makes an ideal hanging planter. A terra-cotta chip prevents the soil from seeping out from the spout. The large cracker bucket,** RIGHT, **will offer this phlox years of happy containment provided there are a few drainage holes added.**

slightly damp but not soggy. When you are not filling containers, place another tarp over the pile to protect it from the elements and keep the moisture level constant. To prevent mold that can develop rather quickly under the covered soil, prepare just enough soil for an hour's worth of work.

Drainage

An old myth in container gardening maintains that as long as you put rocks in the bottom of a container, it doesn't need a drainage hole. Unless you are creating a water garden, that is wrong. Every container holding live plants must have a means for the water to escape. Few containers are porous enough to allow water to evaporate through the walls of the vessel; most will need an actual hole in the bottom.

Depending on the size of the container, drill one ¾-inch-diameter hole in the bottom about every square foot. An old wooden box may already have adequate drainage in crevices left by loose seems. If not, use a drill with a ¾-inch standard bit to make the hole. Drilling drainage holes in stone or terra-cotta containers can be a bit tricky but not impossible. Use a masonry drill bit and wet the surface of the container before drilling. Let the drill do the work, and do not press hard. If it is very difficult to make the hole, the bit may be dull; try a new one.

Bear in mind that there's always a risk of cracking the piece, so if it is a very expensive antique urn (or a piece too precious or too old to devalue with a drainage hole anyway), or if it is glass or some material too breakable or too strong to puncture, you may want to reconsider planting directly in it. Simply place a potted plant inside the beautiful container and voilà! Be sure to put rocks in the bottom of the outer container so that the plant won't be sitting in its own drainage water. Remember also that any container without a drainage hole and all terra-cotta vessels need special care to survive a freezing winter (see "Protecting the Container," page 183).

How to Plant a Wooden Box

Dovetailed wooden boxes make great container gardens, but they tend to pull apart quickly when exposed to moisture, and should always be lined. (If you use a less-precious box, such as a wooden milk crate, you need not line it; in fact, letting the soil and roots "breathe" will help the plants grow.) The steps below are for a potted garden in a lined wooden box.

An old wooden toolbox, LEFT, with its handle intact, is an ideal windowsill garden, planted with big-leafed plants.
1. Before planting a dovetailed wooden box, secure the corners with finishing nails. A box that is nailed together will need additional nails only if it seems weak at the joints.
2. To make sure the box has adequate drainage, use a $^3/_4$-inch standard bit to make a hole in the bottom. Don't skip this step; good drainage is one of the most important factors in the success of your plants.

3. To line the wooden container, cut a generous piece of plastic a good 6 inches larger than the inside surface. Use garbage bags, preferably the kind used by contractors, for the plastic; thinner plastic might tear. If you think you might miscalculate the size of the container, measure the bottom and sides with a ruler before you cut, or simply wrap the bag around the outside of the container to get a rough idea of its dimensions. Press the plastic into the container, then staple it on the inside at the top. (Don't staple it too far down or moisture will leak between the wood and the lining.)

4. Using a large pair of scissors, poke a hole through the lining at the same location as the hole in the bottom of the container. Place a rock or a terra-cotta chip over the hole to prevent the plastic from slipping and clogging the drainage hole. Remember to pierce the lining *before* you put in the soil and the plants.

5. Using premixed, moistened soil, fill the lined box to where the bottom of the new plants will be.

6. Trim the excess plastic, leaving only an inch hanging out around the entire edge.

7. Now you are ready for the plants. If the nursery container is made of cardboard or flexible plastic, loosen the plant by gently squeezing the entire pot. The plant should come out easily unless it is dangerously root bound. Do not force the plant from the container. If it is stuck, cut the plastic or cardboard from the root ball.

1. **To make a hole in a metal container, depending on its thickness and durability, you can pound out the hole with a hammer and awl. If you are the aggressive type, a quick blow with the pointy end of a pickax will do the trick quickly and easily. Be careful not to destroy your container or anyone or anything in your path with too much power or too little control.**

2. **Three generous holes are just right for this fire bucket.**
3. **Place terra-cotta shards over the drainage holes.**
4. **For any containers larger than 1-gallon size, place a couple of inches of pebbles in the bottom before adding the soil; to lighten the load on rooftops or decks, use Styrofoam peanuts. (But don't overdo the Styrofoam; tall trees and perennials need large rocks to anchor them.)**
5. **Pour in a couple of inches of soil, leaving enough room to place your deepest plant.**

How to Plant a Metal Container

Planting in metal containers is a bit different from planting in wood. For one thing, the rust from metal containers can change the pH of the soil enough to kill some plants. Line all rustable metals (and copper containers, as discussed on page 78) using the same method outlined on the preceding pages. A metal container (such as a colander) with so many holes that it won't hold soil or that would allow the soil to drain too quickly can be adapted with sphagnum moss, Spanish moss, or plastic sheeting.

6. Remove the plants from the nursery containers. (See page 143 for details.) Loosen and stimulate the roots of the plants by gently separating and kneading the roots and the soil. Try not to rip the roots; just work them enough for some of the soil to shake loose. Never leave any cardboard or burlap on the root ball, even if the nursery directions suggest that it be planted intact. These materials may break down easily in the ground, but not in a potted garden. And if there is already a shard embedded in the root ball, it should be removed too.

7. Next, ignore the spacing instructions on the nursery label. They are meant to ensure maximum growth over months or years in the ground. Fast and expansive growth is not always desirable in a container garden. A potted garden always looks better when chockful of plants. Position the crown of the plant level with the surface of the soil. Once everything is planted in the container add more soil to all the crevices, gently working it in around the roots and tamping down with your fingers.

8. When you are finished adding the soil, ¹/₂ inch or so of the pot should show around the upper edge to prevent soil runoff. Water thoroughly. About a half hour after watering add more soil to compensate for any settling that may have occurred. If you have lined the container and have not already trimmed the edges, trim back to 1 inch and tuck the lining in around the base of the plants.

9. The finished potted garden will last for years if properly maintained. When it is brought in from the patio for the winter, it will need to be placed over a saucer filled with pebbles to protect floors or furniture. Enjoy!

How to Plant Bulbs

A couple of years ago, I gave all my nongardening friends paperwhite narcissus bulbs for Christmas. An odd assortment of pots, bowls, and boxes held a dozen bulbs, soil, or rocks and a little note with instructions. Two impatient friends gave up within days, but after a few weeks the phone calls began, and you would have thought my friends had given birth.

Growing paperwhite narcissus and amaryllis bulbs in containers is easy. Tulips, daffodils (narcissus species), hyacinths, crocuses, ranunculus, and irises need to be "forced" to bloom, that is chilled below 45° F for 8 to 16 weeks in order to bloom. When planting bulbs in an outdoor container, plant in the fall; at least one month before the first frost date for your zone. Since bulbs bloom at different times, you can orchestrate an entire season by using a variety. Plant tulips about 10 inches deep, cover with 2 inches of soil, plant the hyacinths, add another 2 inches, then plant the crocuses, finishing off with 2 more inches of soil. Water well and place in a cool, damp place (42° F is ideal for tulips). As soon as the top growth is over 1 inch, it is safe to bring them to a sunny windowsill to bloom.

Amaryllis and paperwhites are the easiest bulbs to grow. Amaryllis are potted in soil, with 1 inch of soil around them, and about $2/3$ of the bulb below the soil. If planted around Thanksgiving, they should be ready for Christmas. Keep in a dark damp spot around 60 to 70° F. Paperwhites are even simpler:

1. Choose a container of almost any size and any type, as long as it does not have a hole, since it needs to hold water.
2. Fill about halfway with pebbles or rocks.
3. Nestle the paperwhites over the rocks, placing them tightly together.
4. Water so that the water level comes just to the base of the bulbs.
5. Place in a sunny spot and watch them turn into a a fragrant garden. Keep water level constant so that roots are always moist.

1 2 3

4 5

terrace

from my bedroom, 25 feet from my terrace door, I awaken to the high-pitched squeals of birds fleeing the neighbor's cat. On a canvas recliner, I sip coffee sweetened only by the scent of the lilacs. I while away the morning counting the butterflies on the buddleia and the bees on the sunflowers. If not for the sirens and the horns, I might forget I am in New York City. Not every city dweller can enjoy a terrace roof garden, but if the space is there, it cries out for planting.

A retired baby's bathtub finds a new purpose holding a small perennial garden high atop a roof, ABOVE. My old canvas recliner beckons me each morning to my terrace, OPPOSITE.

The most important consideration when planning a deck garden is whether or not the structure under-

neath will support the garden's weight. If in doubt, an engineer or architect is a good investment. Be warned, however: in my career as a terrace garden designer in New York City, I have found only the most conservative advisers. The first response of all lawyers and most architects or engineers is, "No garden." It is only after much prodding and a detailed explanation of how I reduce the weight of the traditional container garden that some agree. A deck or roof that is built well with the proper supports can withstand the weight of just about any potted garden. But don't be imprudent, either. A tree crashing through a neighbor's ceiling will change the way you feel about your garden for a long time.

First, deck the area fully with pressure-treated cedar or redwood. If the terrace is to be placed on top of a roof, the deck should be designed and built in easily removable sections. If the roof springs a leak, you do not want to have to remove the entire garden and deck to repair it.

Another crucial consideration is the watering plan for your container garden. A few years ago, I was hired to design a grand garden high atop a famous building in the middle of Times Square in

My own terrace, ABOVE, **looked desolate and bare before it had a garden. This view can be seen from my kitchen, so if I had left it like this, it would have made washing the dishes each day nearly impossible.**

New York City. The space was spectacular. I nearly fainted when I first walked out on the roof and saw the view. I imagined that it would be my most incredible garden ever. The problem arose when my clients, who rented their offices, approached the owners of the building about installing a watering system. Oddly enough, the owners had no problem with a garden, but they would not allow any plumbing to be extended to water the garden. My clients begged me to put a garden on the roof nonetheless. Many of the employees volunteered to drag a watering can through all the offices each day. I explained that in good conscience I could not give them a garden with no realistic source of water. I knew that they would never water the garden sufficiently with a heavy watering can, covering the distance of a football field from the bathroom to the terrace, day in and day out. The first few weeks maybe, but not forever.

It is important to have a reliable watering plan for any container garden. In the middle of a hot July, high atop a roof or even on a deck or at poolside, your garden may have to be watered as much as twice a day. It is unrealistic to think that this could be accomplished by using a watering can for each pot. The watering alone could take hours a day. At that point, you no longer have a beautiful garden, you simply have a big burden.

An automatic watering system is a terrific luxury, running anywhere from not too expen-

With more than one hundred odd containers, my terraced roof is transformed into a garden paradise. Each container is moveable by one person so that the roof remains easily accessible.

sive to outrageous. The problem with automatic systems is that each container needs a little tributary hose that attaches to the main line. If your potted garden design calls for 50 or more separate containers, the system can be an unruly solution, with a tremendous potential for leakage. In addition, the individual tributaries are difficult to disguise.

A personal commitment and an ordinary hose is the best watering solution for a con-

The garden landscape, PRECEDING PAGES, **mimics the city skyline. Old chairs with worn seats can be used for climbing vines,** RIGHT. **The colors and textures of copper containers and English washtubs keep a terrace garden earthy.**

tainer garden. Watering can be a great way to relax or meditate. You can also keep a constant vigil for bugs, slugs, and disease during your daily watering ritual. Any garden that does not have a brief daily inspection has a tendency to wither or to become infested with problems. No one said gardening would be completely carefree, but regular care can prevent problems before they happen.

Designing a Terrace Garden

Designing and planting a potted terrace or deck garden is like painting on a very large blank canvas. Some artists sketch out in detail before painting, while others would only be stifled by such an exercise. Even for those who indulge in freehand, some thought for the look and feel of the garden is an essential first step. Whether your plan is drawn up or in your mind, you will need it to make a list of the containers and plants required. If you've never drawn a ground plan before, the easiest way to translate a large space onto a piece of paper is to measure the length and width of your garden-to-be and draw a grid to a ratio of 1 inch for every 1 foot. To represent the plants, cut various-size squares, rectangles, and circles out of sheets of colored paper. Move the bits of paper around the drawing until they make aesthetic and practical sense. Keep in mind the position of your furniture and the angle of the sun.

Judging the amount of sun on a terrace over the course of a year takes almost scientific knowledge. Observation is the best way for most of us to figure out the sunny, shady, and windy spots. The great thing about planting a potted garden is that everything is movable, so if you make a mistake on your sun prediction, don't worry—it is not so difficult to make adjustments.

Ingredients

Once your plants are purchased it is important to plant them as soon as possible. Assemble your tools and materials from the following list before you begin.

- The various-size containers from your garden plan (plus a few extra)
- Enough soil to fill all the containers (if more than 20 cubic feet is needed, mix your own —you'll save a fortune)
- Pebbles and/or Styrofoam pellets for drainage
- Broken terra-cotta pots
- Lots of industrial-strength garbage bags (sold in hardware stores)
- All the plants, seeds, and bulbs
- Two plastic dropcloths
- Hose and watering can
- Garden tools: shovel, trowel, hand fork, clippers, and scissors
- Pickax, hammer, nails, screwdriver, and screws to make container alterations
- Wire and twine to hang objects and to tie up trellising plants
- A few large pails or washtubs to pot smaller things inside of without messing up the whole space
- Rugged, carefree clothes
- A minimum of three hours, depending on the scale of the project (estimate one hour for every five containers)
- A strong back
- Friends and/or family

OPPOSITE, CLOCKWISE FROM ABOVE LEFT: **Every detail of a garden should be as spectacular as the garden as a whole. Echinacea and achillea in a wine crate, cavalhoe sprawling from a galvanized pail, a watering can planted behind a fence, and nasturtiums pouring out of an old copper washtub are just a few elements that make a potted terrace garden.**

Plant Choice

Just about every plant that will grow in the ground where you live will also grow in a pot. So break free of the old geraniums-in-a-row mentality. Do not limit yourself to plants usually recommended for container gardening. Experiment with the ground cover ajuga as a trailing plant, or reed grasses instead of bushes for edging. Mix and match grasses with flowers, perennials with annuals, ground covers with vines, vegetables with roses. Anything goes. On the subject of container plants, nursery advice will not be nearly as helpful as your own good sense. If I had a dime for every time I was told I couldn't grow a particular plant in a container that subsequently flourished, I would be a rich woman today! Rather than asking if something is appropriate for a pot, ask about the plant's needs. Armed with a little information, you will be able to guess whether it will grow well in a deep pot or in

A beautiful iron bed
from days gone by
makes a perfect trellis
for morning glories.

sandy soil, whether it needs to be kept moist or likes lots of food, and so on. The actual proof of container growth potential comes after the planting and the care.

Spread your flowering season out by planting early-spring bloomers such as tulips, crocuses, morning glories, certain daylilies, many climbing roses, lilies of the valley, violets, and pansies. Mid-summer showoffs include sunflowers, echinacea, rudbeckia, coreopsis, loosestrife, and peonies, followed by a fall of mums, asters, and clematis. Any garden will look more cohesive with a few favorite plants repeated several times throughout the entire space. A mass of the same flowers is often a much more appealing or powerful statement than dozens of varieties of individual plants. This is particularly true with annuals. Pick just a few favorites and buy plenty of flats of each.

Trellises

Most gardens will need some amount of staking and filling in throughout the growing season. Unfortunately, the majority of store-bought trellising and staking methods often produce an eyesore. For every unattractive object designed to support a flower, there is an attractive alternative.

Staking or trellising is a necessity for any potentially tall plant in a windy area. When you are hunt-

Combine fast-growing beanstalks and morning glories with the slower climbing rose for a lush trellis, RIGHT. **The discarded ladder,** OPPOSITE, **makes an ideal support for any climber.**

ing for the containers for your garden, also look for appealing objects that can serve as garden stakes for tall or climbing plants. Antique iron headboards, wooden ladders, and old metal gates are beautiful and functional. The popularity of old metal bed frames has resurged tremendously in the past few years, but the headboard sold without the foot or the frame is still affordable and all that is needed for the garden.

The simplest and most natural staking solution is to use one plant to hold up another. This is particularly helpful in a container garden, where space is usually at a premium—the more plants that are used to solve problems, the better. Taller and stronger plants can support tender climbers and wind-sensitive perennials. It is important, though, to watch the balance of the two plants carefully. A climbing plant allowed to grow unchecked will strangle its helpful neighbor.

It is not always easy to figure out how to secure a stake in a container garden. If the pot is deep enough, the soil alone may anchor it in place, but most potted garden containers will not be deep enough to hold a heavy stake. Sometimes the pots can be gathered tightly enough around a stake to support it, and walls and pipes can hold a leaning makeshift trellis if it can be secured with wire so the wind won't blow it over. The sand-filled bases sold for patio umbrellas will hold a pole or broomstick, but these can take up a lot of "floor space."

Planting vertically allows you to create gardens in an area with little ground space. Try an untraditional method of growing climbing plants for a lush overgrown look— plant many climbing plants in a single container. Beans, morning glories, and climbing roses make a great combination. The beans grow fast, filling in the gaps of the slower-growing roses and the often thin foliage of the morning glories. But beware: Beanstalks can become so invasive that they will wrap around anything nearby. Be ruthless in tearing away unwanted growth. After a few weeks, big green leaves will again cover an entire wall.

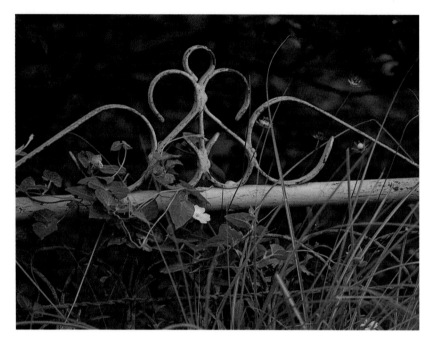

Old garden gates make
ideal trellises and great
neighbors, LEFT. Instead
of shunning old heating
vents and discarded win-
dows, RIGHT, use them as
an accent to any roof
garden. Use the colors
and lines of the archi-
tectural pieces to help
define the space.
FOLLOWING PAGES: **Juniper
topiaries planted in old
English washtubs give
an air of sophistication
to an urban terrace.**

Architectural Objects

Architectural objects and other artifacts can be
used in the garden to add charm, to separate
plants from the walkway, or to draw focus to a
particular area. Garden designer and antique
shop owner Michael Trapp uses Greek urns
and columns as an architectural focus
throughout his garden in West Cornwall, Connecticut. He seldom plants anything in them
that might compete with either the piece or the
natural beauty surrounding his home.

As more and more old buildings are sadly
replaced by sleek high-rises and office com-
plexes, spectacular architectural objects beckon
acts of preservation. Cor-
nices and chunks of wall and
columns that once adorned
these edifices can be planted in the garden to
add beauty and structure. Objects made out of
stone are particularly desirable, because they
age well: the stone softens and moss and lichen
creep along every crevice. To hurry the moss-
ing process, spread a little yogurt on the stone
and keep it damp. Within weeks, your friends
will think you own a piece of the Parthenon.
Succulents and bromeliads can also be grown
out of the crevices of stone objects, because
they require so little soil and water to survive.

My Favorite Climbing and Hanging Plants

- Climbing roses
- Ivy
- Nasturtium
- Morning glories
- Gloxinia climber
- Scarlet runner beans
- Creeping fig
- Trumpet vine
- Ajuga
- Lobelia
- Thunbergia
- Grapevines
- Jasmine
- Sweet pea

Planting

Once you have assembled your tools, containers, and plants, the artistry can begin. But first prepare all the containers with the necessary drainage holes and lining. Place a terra-cotta chip over all the holes, and add any pebbles or Styrofoam needed (see page 144) and a few inches of soil to every pot you plan to use. In the midst of the creative process of placing and planting, it can be distracting to be continually interrupted by the preparation steps.

Plant all the trees first. Likely to be your largest pieces, they will help to define the architectural landscape of the garden. Once you've placed the trees, keeping considerations of sun, design, and sitting comfort in mind, let your creative juices flow. If you have sunny

and shady spots in your garden, organize your plants into groups of sun and shade varieties. Group most of the containers around the trees, with the tallest up against the tree containers, scaling down in a random artful arrangement.

Following the same principle used in cut-flower arranging, odd numbers of pots will look better than even amounts. Now simply place the plants, still in their nursery pots, in all the containers. Think of each container as its own separate garden. Use height, color, and texture to create a miniature landscape in each container. Each individual container should be as visually stimulating on its own as it is in its contribution to the whole.

Stand back and assess your work. If you like it, plant it. If not, keep adjusting until it works. If night begins to fall, perhaps you are overthinking.

String and weather vanes can serve dual purposes in the garden, holding climbing vines as well as adding definition and focus to a space.

epilogue

a gardener's garden is the window to his soul. Potted gardeners are a courageous, pioneering sort who engage in the often vain pursuit of trying to contain nature. As I look back over pictures of my 20 years of gardens, I am reminded of the most important moments of my life. I see old friends in the faces of the blossoms and remember exactly where I was when I found that old copper washtub. Signs of temporary unemployment show in the overpruning of a lilac tree, and clearly I was traveling a lot the summer my garden looked so neglected. On the shore of the small lake where my mother learned to swim, I planted a garden of verbena and rudbeckia in an old wooden boat. A simple tribute to one who died too young.

My garden has always  reflected who I am and where I am in life. In my most chaotic days, my garden is overgrown and underfed. When I seek solitude, my garden becomes rather sparse and uncomplicated. When my garden is busy with color and furniture, my life is surely crazy and full of parties and friends. During the saddest moments of my life, my garden begins to wither away.

I cherish all the stages, as I know my garden has grown with me. Gardening is a way to return to the earth, remember what is real, and experience the power and beauty of nature.

Potted gardening, in particular, depends on the wit and charm of the gardener. Anyone who attempts a container garden must keep in mind that nature will always resist containment. To keep it up you must be forever diligent in its care. If you are, it will return the favor a hundred times over.

Gardening books and catalogs are terrific teachers. Devour information; the more you 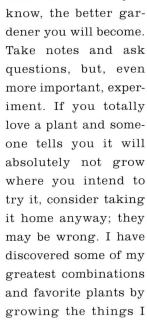 know, the better gardener you will become. Take notes and ask questions, but, even more important, experiment. If you totally love a plant and someone tells you it will absolutely not grow where you intend to try it, consider taking it home anyway; they may be wrong. I have discovered some of my greatest combinations and favorite plants by growing the things I was told would not grow. Learn all you can about the needs of each of your plants, but pay some attention to your heart. There is no need to make gardening and growing your life's work. Most of us are, after all, amateur gardeners. And, as my grandmother always reminded me, the Latin root of "amateur" means "for the love of." There could not be a better reason to garden.

maintaining your potted garden

i love the way gardening books say things like, "In cold areas arums [calla lilies] in clay pots can be overwintered under glass." Anyone who cares enough about calla lilies to build a conservatory is welcome to them. That plant would have to become more important than the favorite family pet for me to treat it with such affection. For at least ten good months of the year, a calla will not bloom and tends to turn a little mangy. Of course, plants deserve every reasonable chance for survival and good health, but as in every aspect of life, we also need to watch the extremes. We ask too much of ourselves, our plants, and our environment if we expect to keep every plant year in, year out.

At least once a week a neighbor or friend leaves an awful-looking plant in front of my apartment door (most call me the "plant lady" because they can't remember my name). As with the orphans of folklore, a little note accompanies each bedraggled specimen, requesting that I call the owner when I have revived it. The patients are usually confined in a hideous plastic contraption that should be replaced immediately with terra cotta, wood, or tin. My home has become a plant shelter for every neglected, underfed, abused plant. They often line my windowsill, announcing to passersby that the residence is not occupied by a "green thumb." If I had actually purchased any of these plants, and had allowed them to get to such a sorry state, I would have discarded them all without a moment's hesitation.

Sometimes I think that sick plants are left as a test of my horticultural skill—and it is not a test I particularly enjoy.

Not knowing the growing habits of every plant should not preclude taking pleasure from it. Regardless of horticultural education, everyone can benefit from nurturing a plant. In the natural cycle of things, a weaker specimen may succumb, but don't be too quick to label yourself a "brown thumb." In fact, some gardens should be viewed as extended cut-flower arrangements. When we make a cut-flower arrangement, we know it will last only four or five days, but when we own a plant, no matter what growing environment it might need, we expect it to last forever.

If you want to have a garden and you don't have a lot of time to care for it, take steps to minimize your efforts. Try to be very loose and carefree about what actually happens in your garden. If a plant dies, don't go with it. That's life. Would-be gardeners whose plant anxiety is high should choose easy-maintenance plants from the succulent, cactus, or ivy family—and try to relax.

Watering

The key requisites for every plant are water, light, food, and soil. Although plants differ in their specific requirements, there are some common elements. Every plant needs water; how much and how often depends on many factors. One of the most common questions of any staff at my store is, "How often should I water this?" The variables are too great to answer that question simply. Most indoor and outdoor plants like to have a regular cycle of moist to dry, but depending on a host of possible influences, such as the weather (hot and dry, for example), a plant may need more watering at one time than another. To water a potted garden properly, bring the container to the sink and really drench the plants until the water pours out of the drainage holes. If the container is wood, its entire bottom will be wet, so be careful returning the wet container to wooden furniture. If you cannot find a tray the appropriate size to fit under a potted garden, dry off the bottom after watering and place the container on a plate of tiles. When a potted garden contains a variety of plants with different watering needs, carefully water each plant individually according to its needs.

Food

All plants need food to survive. They live on a combination of large doses of nitrogen, phosphorus, and potassium and smaller helpings of iron, calcium, manganese, and magnesium. A plant found in nature is fed by its environment. Plants in a pot need to be fed regularly to thrive.

Like people, some plants prefer more of some things and less of others, but for many an even dose of nitrogen, phosphorus, and potassium every couple of weeks will be sufficient. The easiest way to feed your plants is with a good store-bought timed-release capsule. If any plant requires more of one of the three primary nutrients, these can be found naturally. Manure contains plenty of nitrogen, bonemeal is quite high in phosphorus, and eggshells are packed with potassium. For all three nutrients, stir up a witches' brew of fish meal, hoof and horn meal or blood meal, and bonemeal.

The most common signs of malnutrition are yellow foliage and slow growth. The feeding cycle of each plant usually fluctuates according to its growth cycle. Permanent trees and shrubs grow rapidly and continuously. Because most containers will not be big enough to hold any bush or tree at its full growth, withhold its food to slow it down, but don't malnourish. Feed at least on a regular monthly basis.

Perennials in a pot last three to four years on average. They generally have rather shallow root systems and are considered fast growing. They should be fed about twice a month from spring through midsummer, then once a month through the fall and only once more in the winter.

Alpines and evergreens are slow-growing plants requiring very little feeding. Every two months should be sufficient.

Annuals are temporary visitors to the garden. Like most weekend guests, they are hungry often. These fast growers have only half a season to develop a full root system, so feed them once a week throughout their entire growing season. In return, they will produce abundant blooms.

The plants that feed us need to be fed the most. Food crops, such as vegetables, are the hungriest of all plants. They need nitrogen to grow to maturity, followed by potassium to produce fruit. High-potassium tomato fertilizers are great for many flowering and fruit-producing plants as well.

A tightly planted window box will require more regular feedings than any in-the-ground plants. Throughout the blooming season of the garden, feed once a week with a diluted version of liquid plant food; use about one-third of the recommended amount. On the plus side, by planting close together, you eliminate the need for a mulch. The plants themselves will crowd out weeds and will help to keep the soil evenly moist. Don't forget to water your window garden even in the winter, albeit a lot less often than in the summer—perhaps only once a month.

Pruning and Cutting Back

Many plants and trees do better if they are cut back at least once a year. Some prefer to be pruned in the fall, while others do better if pruned just after flowering in the spring. Cutting back a plant encourages new healthy shoots to form and either bloom more often or fill out more fully. Some potted trees and shrubs will need their roots trimmed as well as their branches in order to stay compact enough for a container. Naturally, pruning a full-size tree is a cumbersome and difficult process, so avoid such high maintenance by choosing dwarf varieties of a favorite tree. Since they are bred to stay small, dwarf trees do not need to be cut back very often and won't outgrow their pots so quickly.

The art of careful pruning is similar to the art of fine living—there are many ways to arrive at the result. When cutting back a rose or a flowering plant once the flowers have withered, make the cuts at the fork of a stem and a leaf. Never leave any exposed stem at the end of the last branch. For the majority of flowering plants, the next bud will bloom at the vortex of the fork. Never let dead leaves or branches remain on a plant or in the soil of a container garden. Decaying debris from many plants can alter the acidity of the soil, foster mildew, and attract insects.

Pinch back plant tips to stimulate new growth and more blossoms and to prevent disease. "Deadhead" the seed pockets of most annuals and some perennials by nipping off all spent blossoms. Pansies and petunias can flourish from spring through fall if no blossom is allowed to go to seed. Otherwise the plants become scraggly and leggy, wasting their energy producing seeds rather than blossoms. Climbing plants can often be quite difficult to cut back carefully because their nature is to wind around everything. They are typically rather invasive plants, so rip away; if a climber took over an area once, it is bound to take over again.

Most new gardeners are shy about cutting back a plant and then wonder why the plants in the flower shop and nursery look so much better. Be ruthless and cut back any dead, dying, and overgrown foliage. Your plants will thank you with a big flourish.

Transplanting

Congratulations! If you have progressed far enough to need this topic, you have a successful potted garden. Almost all plants will have to be transplanted someday if they live long enough in a container. Some plants may take years to outgrow their homes; others will become too big in the course of one growing season. And almost any plant grown in plastic will benefit both aesthetically and horticulturally from being transplanted from plastic into a more porous container from the minute you bring it home.

Some plants demand a very strict transplanting schedule. Ficus trees, for instance, respond quite poorly to transplanting soon after a big move. So even though that ugly plastic pot is an eyesore when you first bring it home from the store, resist transplanting the tree into your grandmother's old washtub for three weeks or so. Ming aralias seem to die anytime you transplant them, so if you want to grow one, plop the ugly container inside a more attractive one.

Most plants, however, respond quite well to transplanting. If you are unsure about any particular plant, consult the place where you purchased it or your local botanical garden.

The two basic rules of thumb to follow when transplanting are:

1. Try not to move a plant in the middle of its growing and blooming season. Early spring and midfall are often the best times to make the move.

2. If you live in the North, do not transplant outdoor plants just before the big frost. The roots of any plant will be at least somewhat traumatized by the disturbance, so they will need to settle into their new home before their world freezes over.

Transplanting will become necessary when one or more plants in a container grow significantly faster than the others and begin to overcrowd them. Despite the first basic rule, smaller sun-loving plants may become too shaded by tall plants by midseason, and it is better to risk transplanting them, since they may die if left alone. In the middle of a July heat wave, you'll have to use your judgment about which course of action will be best for the plant.

Outdoor transplanting is best done in the late afternoon. Once the plants are nestled in their new home, water very well. The cooler night air will help keep plants moist for as long as possible. If you must transplant early in the day, water again in the afternoon lest the sun has dried out the roots and the soil. Never transplant at high noon.

Pests

The ants go marching two by two. Every gardener will have to contend with bugs and fungal diseases at some point. If bugs occur, don't be discouraged or act too hastily.

A few years ago, good friends of mine bought their first house. With it came a huge overgrown garden. Now, mind you, these were friends who only a year before, when I presented them with a potted garden, cried and asked me to take it back because they feared killing it. Three months or so into their new gardening adventure, aphids appeared throughout most of the garden. Although the invasion appeared to them to have occurred overnight, the aphids probably had been feeding for quite some time: the instinct to look for unwanted critters was not yet in these pioneer gardeners. My friends are usually the all-natural type, but they were nevertheless seized with the impulse to run out and buy the most poisonous spray they could find. After some consoling from all their gardening friends, they tried a less toxic method and conquered the aphids well before the aphids destroyed the garden.

The basic thing to keep in mind about pests is that they are both inevitable and preventable. This might sound contradictory at first, but let me explain. Bugs love dead or neglected plants. The healthier your plants, the less likely it is that they will attract unwanted pests. That said, bugs and mildews should not be seen as a sign of bad gardening; every garden will succumb once in a while. The important thing is to keep your wits about you.

The No-Chemical Approach

Healthy, watered, and well-fed plants are the best prevention against the need for chemicals to fight pests. Pick off all dead leaves and never leave rotting plant material on the soil. There is a common misconception that dead leaves will feed a plant. In order for dead leaves to become truly beneficial, they need to be broken down by earthworms or the compost heap. Worms are usually not crawling around in the soil of potted plants.

Since potted gardens are normally small and are frequently indoors, try washing or picking bugs off before trying anything else. Caterpillars, sawfly grubs, some aphids, and pollen beetles can all be removed by hand. If the bugs are tiny and plentiful, sandwich the affected leaf or stem between damp cloths and gently wash them away.

Choosing the right plants for your environment will deter infestation. Many favorite plants have been bred to be disease resistant. Ask your local nursery expert to direct you toward those choices. Some plants also have natural disease-fighting chemicals. Combining the proper plants that can help one another is also very effective. Tomatoes and other vegetables, for instance, are prone to a number of maladies that can be deterred by underplanting with marigolds.

Chemical Warfare

Use chemicals in moderation. Gardens are intended to enhance our environment, not destroy it, and exposure to poisons is not so good for the gardener either. If you must use chemicals, try natural-based ones such as derris dust (rotenone), copper sulfates, and calcium hydroxide. A plant that does not respond to a small amount of low-grade chemicals should be tossed out.

As your doctor has told you, there are no known cures for viruses. It is not always easy to determine when a plant has developed a virus, but if a perfectly healthy-looking specimen begins to deteriorate quickly for no apparent reason, a virus may be the culprit. Aphids carry viruses, so it is particularly important to eradicate them as soon as they appear.

Good Bugs versus Bad Bugs

Just as there are good witches and bad witches, there are good bugs and bad bugs. Some bugs can kill some other bugs. Some popular "good" insects are lacewings, praying mantises, and ladybugs, which devour aphids. But note that insects don't stay where you put them. Once they have run out of food, they will "fly away home." And indoors, well . . . not everyone will find your new pets as interesting as you do.

Winterizing

If you live in a climate zone that drops below freezing for more than a day, you will need to put some of your garden to bed. This process will help protect the roots and branches of your perennial flowers, trees, and shrubs. The time to do this is before a deep, long-lasting frost destroys some of your containers or the plants —usually from about mid-October to the beginning of December, depending on how far north you live.

Take indoors all the plants you want to keep that won't survive the winter outdoors. Many annuals that will not make it through a deep frost may not appreciate the unchanging heat of the inside of a home either. Most plants like to be cool at night and have plenty of ventilation at all times—not always the climate inside our homes. The best way to find out if a plant will do well indoors is to try it. Experiment over-wintering ground covers and annuals, but remember that annuals usually get too leggy or buggy soon after coming indoors. Do not become discouraged if your beautiful potted petunias must be discarded after the first week of the experiment.

The perennials that remain outdoors can be divided into two basic categories: hardy and half-hardy. The real hardy ones will be okay just hanging out in the freezing cold. The others will need to be wrapped with plastic for protection from the wind and the severe cold. Roses should be wrapped up to about 6 inches above the soil to protect the bud union (the place on the stem where the hybrid variety was grafted onto the rootstock).

For hardy plants and bulbs, freezing is not what causes the damage in a container; the killer is the quick and continuous freeze-thaw cycle. Put bubble wrap and burlap around the entire container to make a kind of thermos. Once the root ball is cold it will stay cold, and even a sudden thaw will take a while to reach the plant's roots.

Moisture and drainage are as important in the winter as in the summer. Keep the drainage hole open and the pots slightly raised above the ground. Your plants will need less water in winter, but they will need some. Keep a watchful eye, and water if there is a winter drought.

Protecting the Container

As much fun as it is to hunt for new containers for your potted garden, you won't want to replace every one of them each year. If you live in an area that freezes part of the winter, most containers will have to be protected from the elements.

Terra-cotta planters run a high risk of crack-ing because they are porous, meaning they have air spaces in the sand that is fired to make them. Water seeps through the tiny air bubbles, and if it freezes, the water expands and cracks the pot. One way to minimize (but not eliminate) the pos-sibility of cracking is to wrap the sides of the pot with bubble wrap. Plants need to be watered and continue to drain throughout the winter, so do not wrap the top or bottom of the container with the plastic.

To finish the job, wrap the bubble wrap with burlap. The burlap can cover the bottom because the water will pass right through it. Tie the top of the material with heavy twine, leaving 8 inches flapping in the wind. Untie the twine when it's time to water.

Glossary

Acid soil Soil with a pH level less than 7. *See* pH.

Alkaline soil Soil with a pH level greater than 7.

Alpine A plant native to a climate zone that is above the timberline; a plant from a mountainous region that may also thrive in low altitudes, often used in rock gardens.

Analogous colors Harmonious, related hues that appear close to each other on a color wheel, such as yellow, yellow-green, and green.

Annual A plant that completes its life cycle (germination, flowering, seed production, death) in one growing season.

Aphid Any of numerous small insects that suck the juices of plants.

Automatic watering system An often expensive alternative to the hose or watering can, consisting of tributary hoses, sprinklers, or channels that bring water throughout a garden.

Awl A pointed tool similar to an ice pick for marking surfaces or piercing holes.

Bonsai A potted plant that is dwarfed and shaped by specialized pruning methods.

Bromeliad A tropical, epiphytic herbaceous plant that derives its nutrients from the air and rain and that usually lives mounted on another plant; includes such plants as Spanish moss.

Bubble wrap A plastic packing material in sheet form that incorporates rows of encapsulated air pockets. The cushions of trapped air can be used in gardening to insulate a plant's roots and protect them from dramatic temperature changes.

Bulb A compact, fleshy, more or less separate organ of a plant (such as a lily, onion, or tulip) that is usually formed underground and consists of a short base bearing one or more buds enclosed in overlapping fleshy leaves.

Calcium A silver-white metallic element of the alkaline-earth group used as a nutrient for plants.

Climate zone A geographical region in which topographic factors, such as mountains and coasts, affect conditions of temperature, rainfall, humidity, and so forth and consequently the growing season. The four main climate zones are the tropical, desert, temperate, and polar.

Complementary colors Contrasting colors that are opposite each other on the color wheel, such as yellow and purple.

Copper sulfate A white powdery or blue crystalline deposit often used as an algicide or fungicide.

Cornice A molded horizontal decorative element that crowns a column.

Cutting A portion of a plant, such as a stem, root, or bud, that is cut to start a new plant.

Cutting back Trimming a plant, often just below a growth bud or at the plant's base.

Deadheading The removal of dead or dying blooms and seed pockets to prevent the plant from going to seed and to encourage continuous blooming.

Derris dust A poisonous preparation made from derris roots and stems used as an insecticide.

Dormant bare-root plant A plant temporarily in a nongrowth period that is handled with the roots not in soil, hence "bare-root."

Dovetailing A series of cuts on two pieces of wood made so that they fit together tightly in an interlocking manner resembling the feathers of a dove's tail.

Drainage The passage, or the system of passage, of excess water through soil.

Drought-resistant plant A plant that requires less frequent watering, such as a succulent.

Dwarf A plant much below normal size, often produced through breeding or by cultivation methods such as root trimming.

Established roots A system of well-developed roots able to withstand conditions outside the nursery.

Evergreen A plant whose leaves remain and stay green throughout the winter.

Fertilizers A material that is added to the soil for its nutritive benefit for plant growth.

Fish meal Ground dried fish and fish waste used as a fertilizer.

Flea market An open-air market for secondhand articles and antiques.

Food crops Vegetables.

Forcing Inducing a plant's growth through artificial control of its environment, usually through changes of temperature and light.

Freeze/thaw cycle A period of freezing temperatures followed by a warmer period, which can cause significant root and container damage. Since container plants are not as well insulated by surrounding earth as are plants in the ground, they are especially susceptible to this type of damage.

Frost date A date when freezing is likely to occur in a region.

Fungal disease A disease caused by parasitic plants such as molds, rusts, mildews, and yeasts.

Goldman, Emma (1869–1940) Lithuanian-born international anarchist and radical feminist. Activist, author, flower lover, and originator of the quote "If I can't dance, I don't want to be a part of your revolution."

Ground cover A low-growing plant that spreads quickly and covers the ground.

Hardy plant A plant able to withstand year-round climatic conditions.

Hoof and horn meal Ground hooves and horns, high in nitrogen, used as a fertilizer.

Horticulture The science of growing fruits, vegetables, flowers, or ornamental plants.

Hue A slight variation of the same color; the attribute by which a color is classified on the color wheel or in the spectrum.

Humus Organic/vegetable remains (compost) used to create fertile soil mixtures.

Indigenous plant A plant naturally occurring in a particular region or environment.

Irish stretch A story told to establish a belief, often for the benefit of the storyteller, usually based on a true circumstance but greatly blown out of proportion.

Iron A nutrient used to develop proteins required for plant growth; a silver-white metallic element that readily oxidizes, forming rust.

Junkaholic One who loses self-control in the purchase of junk. Usually found at flea markets, tag sales, and antiques stores with overloaded arms and car trunk; often leaves with an empty wallet.

Junk-hunting season That period of time between Labor Day and Thanksgiving in the northeastern United States when bargain hunters scour the secondhand markets.

Lacewing An insect with delicate lacelike wings, long antennae, and bright eyes that feeds on aphids.

Lichen Any of numerous plants made up of an alga and a fungus growing in symbiotic association on a solid surface such as a rock.

Magnesium A silver-white metallic element used as a nutrient to develop proteins required for plant growth.

Manganese A grayish white metallic element used as a nutrient to develop proteins required for plant growth.

Manure Livestock excreta often used as a fertilizer.

Masonry drill bit A drill bit designed to cut

through brick, terra cotta, and tile, usually diamond tipped.

Microclimate The conditions that exist in a particular garden that differ from those predominating locally, such as areas of shade, wind tunnels, or wind blockage.

Mulch A protective covering spread on the ground to reduce evaporation, to maintain even soil temperature, to prevent erosion, to control weeds, or to enrich the soil.

Neutral soil Soil with a pH level of 7.

Nitrogen A nutrient used to develop proteins required for plant growth.

Objet d'art An object or article of artistic or decorative value.

Palette A particular range, quality, or use of color. *See* Tight palette.

Peat Partially decayed plant matter rich in humus, formed on the surface of waterlogged soils, commonly used in soil mixes for its nutrient content.

Perennial A plant that lives for at least three seasons.

Perlite Volcanic glass expanded by heat to form a lightweight aggregate used to aerate potting soil.

pH A scale expressing hydrogen activity, which is used in horticulture to describe the acidity or alkalinity of soil. On a scale from 1 to 14, pH 1 is the most acidic, 7 represents neutrality, and 14 indicates the most alkaline.

Phosphorus A nonmetallic element of the nitrogen family; an organic compound used as a fertilizer.

Pickax An iron tool, pointed on one side and flat on the other, useful for making drainage holes in large metal containers.

Pinching back The removal of a growing tip by hand to induce side shoots.

Porous Permeable to liquid. Wood is an example of a porous material.

Potassium A silver-white soft metallic element of the alkali group used as a plant nutrient.

Potted garden A container planted as a full miniature garden.

Potting soil A mixture of soil, sand, peat, or other ingredients in which container plants are grown.

Praying mantis An insect that feeds on other insects and clasps its prey in forelimbs held up as if in prayer.

Pressure-treated wood Wood processed with chemicals to increase its durability and water resistance.

Primary colors The three colors, specifically red, yellow, and blue, from which all other colors may be derived.

Prune To reduce by eliminating superfluous matter to allow for more fruitful growth or to improve the shape of a plant.

Rocky soil A dry, free-draining, often infertile soil.

Root ball The essential roots and accompanying soil of a plant removed from a container or the earth.

Root-bound A term used to describe a condition of tightly wound, congested root that results from leaving a plant too long in too small a container.

Root space The area beneath a plant's roots required for healthy propagation; varies from plant to plant.

Sandy soil A dry, light, free-draining, often infertile soil.

Sap bucket A container used to collect the sap of maple trees, from which syrup and sugar are made.

Sawfly grub A plant-eating larva resembling a caterpillar.

Secondary color A color, such as orange, green, or purple, formed by mixing primary colors in equal quantities.

Seed The fertilized ovule of a plant capable of germination to produce a new plant.

Seed starter A container often made from peat in which seedlings are grown.

Shade garden A garden that contains plants that can thrive with little or no direct sunlight.

Shoot New plant growth.

Sour soil Acidic soil, preferred by woodland plants.

Staking Supporting a tender plant. *See* Trellis.

Stock A plant used to obtain seeds or cuttings to create new plants.

Styrofoam peanuts A packing material useful in container gardening for reducing weight and improving drainage.

Succulent A plant, such as a cactus, having fleshy tissue designed to conserve moisture.

Sulfur compounds Chemicals used in pest and disease control.

Sweet soil Alkaline soil, preferred by succulents, herbs, and green grass lawns.

Symmetry Balanced proportions; a correspondence in size or placement.

Tag sale A sale of used goods, also known as a yard or garage sale. Tag sales evoke joys and perils similar to those of flea markets. *See* Flea market; Junkaholic.

Tight palette A close range of colors and hues.

Topsoil The uppermost, fertile layer of soil.

Toxic Poisonous.

Trailing plant A plant that produces long stems that grow over or pass between other stems or branches and that attach loosely, if at all.

Transplant To lift and reset in another soil or container.

Trellis An object used as a support for climbing plants.

Tributary hose A smaller channeling hose extending from a main hose and used to bring water to a system of plants.

Tropical plant A plant indigenous to the region 23½° north and south of the equator that is characterized by high temperatures and heavy, seasonal rains.

Tuber A short, fleshy, underground stem with the potential of producing a new plant.

Underplant To plant low-growing plants underneath larger plants.

Variegated A term used to describe leaves having distinct markings of different colors; for example, green leaves with white or yellow designs.

Vermiculite A lightweight, highly water-absorbent material composed of granules of heat-expanded mica.

Water garden Any of a wide range of water settings with complementing flowers and foliage.

Water plant A plant that requires a water environment in which to grow ranging from moist soil to deep water.

Weed A plant that is not valued where it is growing.

Wildflower The flower of any uncultivated plant.

Recommended Readings and Other Sources

Antiques and Collectibles

BOOKS

AUCTION ACTION. Ralph Roberts. Blue Ridge Summit, Pa.: TAB Books, 1986.
How to get the best buys and avoid the perils at any type of auction. Covers all types of sales.

BARGAINS, DEALS AND STEALS. Brian G. Marshall. Salt Lake City: Discovery Publications, 1991.
Inside information on house sales, farm sales, estate sales, auctions, antiques, and housewares.

FLEA MARKET TREASURES. Dan D'Imperio. Blue Ridge Summit, Pa.: TAB Books.
Gives full descriptions of hundreds of different collectibles, the current market value of items, what buys to avoid, and more.

GARAGE SALE AND FLEA MARKET ANTIQUES. Paducah, Ky.: Collector Books, annually.
Outlines garage sales, auctions, flea markets, and tag sales. Comprehensive price lists include the current value of today's collectibles.

OFFICIAL DIRECTORY OF U.S. FLEA MARKETS. Kitty Werner, ed. New York: House of Collectibles, annually.
Lists hundreds of flea markets nationwide—the large and small, Alaska to Maine—and selected Canadian markets. Includes merchandise types, changing venues, parking fees, admission charges, and facilities.

RUMMAGER'S HANDBOOK. R. S. McClurg. Pownal, Vt.: Storey Communications.
Finding, buying, cleaning, fixing, using, and selling secondhand treasures.

PERIODICALS

THE ANTIQUE PRESS. 12403 North Florida Ave., Tampa, FL 33612.

ANTIQUE REVIEW. P.O. Box 538, Washington, OH 43085, (614) 885-9757.

ANTIQUE WEEK. P.O. Box 90, Knightstown, IN 46148, (317) 345-5133.

ANTIQUES AND THE ARTS WEEKLY. The Newtown Bee, Newtown, CT 06470, (203) 426-8036.

ANTIQUES AND COLLECTIBLES. Good Times Magazine, P.O. Box 33, Westbury, NY 11590, (516) 334-9650.

COLLECTIBLES: FLEA MARKET FINDS. GCR Publishing Group, Inc., 1700 Broadway, New York, NY 10019, (800) 955-3870.

Gardeners' Resources

BOOKS

THE AMERICAN HORTICULTURAL ENCYCLOPEDIA OF GARDENING. Christopher Brickell, ed. New York: Dorling Kindersley, 1993.
The comprehensive guide to landscaping and gardening techniques.

THE CITY AND TOWN GARDENER. Linda Yang. New York: Random House, 1990.
A handbook for planting in small spaces and containers, including resources for all container-gardening needs.

THE CONTAINER GARDEN. Nigel Colborn; photographs by Marijke Heuff. New York: Crescent Books, 1990.
Successful plant and container choices from terra-cotta pots to sinks. Outlines usage on balconies, roof terraces, windowsills, and more. Discusses container integration into existing gardens.

THE ESSENTIAL GARDENER. Derek Fell. New York: Crescent Books, 1990.

A detailed sourcebook for annuals, perennials, bulbs, roses, trees, shrubs, herbs, and vegetables.

THE GARDEN PROBLEM SOLVER. Catriona Tudor Erler; photographs by Jerry Pavia. New York: Simon & Schuster, 1994.
Offers 101 solutions to common landscaping problems.

GARDENING BY MAIL. Barbara J. Barton. Boston: Houghton Mifflin, 1994.
A mail-order sourcebook for everything from antiques to wildflowers.

THE INDOOR POTTED BULB. Rob Proctor; photographs by Lauren Springer and Rob Proctor. New York: Simon & Schuster, 1993.
Describes bulbs that will successfully thrive indoors year-round and gives home decorating ideas and horticultural advice.

MÄDDERLAKE'S TRADE SECRETS. Tom Pritchard and Billy Jarecki; photographs by Langdon Clay and Tom Pritchard. New York: Clarkson N. Potter, 1994.
Finding and arranging flowers naturally.

NEW FLOWER ARRANGING. Jane Packer; photographs by Peter Williams. North Pomfret, Vt.: Trafalgar Square Publishing, 1994.
Includes seasonal floral selections and combinations, container recommendations, information on plant material and equipment, and plant-care glossary.

THE OUTDOOR POTTED BULB. Rob Proctor; photographs by Lauren Springer and Rob Proctor. New York: Simon & Schuster, 1993.
Covers plant combinations, climate considerations, light requirements, and design.

RANDOM HOUSE BOOK OF PERENNIALS: VOLUME 2, *Late Perennials.* Roger Phillips and Martin Rix. New York: Random House, 1994.
Covers late-summer and autumn-flowering plants in a variety of settings, including dry Mediterranean, woodland, meadow and prairie, lakeside, and swamps, and border gardens. Offers planting guidelines.

TAYLOR'S GUIDE TO CONTAINER GARDENING. Roger Holmes, ed.; Frances Tenenbaum, series ed. Boston: Houghton Mifflin, 1995.
Practical care for container gardens, landscaping strategies, and proper plant and container selection.

PERIODICALS

FINE GARDENING. Taunton Press, P.O. Box 5506, 63 South Main St., Newtown, CT 06470.

HORTICULTURE: THE MAGAZINE OF AMERICAN GARDENING. Horticulture Ltd. Partnership, 20 Park Plaza, Suite 1220, Boston, MA 02116.

SUPPPLIES, POTS, AND PLANTS

A. M. Leonard, Inc., P.O. Box 816, Piqua, OH 45356, (800) 543-8955.

Conley's Garden Center, 145 Townsend Ave., Boothbay Harbor, ME 04538, (207) 633-5020.

Eastern Shore Pottery, U.S. 13, Capeville, VA 23313, (804) 331-2505.

Indoor Gardening Supplies, P.O. Box 40567, Detroit, MI 48240, (313) 426-9080.

The Kinsman Company, River Rd., Point Pleasant, PA 18950, (800) 733-4146.

Natural Gardening Company, 217 San Anselmo Ave., San Anselmo, CA 94960, (707) 766-9303.

Patio Garden Ponds, 7919 S. Shields, Oklahoma City, OK 73149, (405) 634-7663.

Syracuse Pottery, 6551 Pottery Rd., Warners, NY 13164, (315) 487-6066.

Index

Potted Gardens

27 Bedford Street

New York, New York 10014

212 255-4797 Fax 212 255-4680